NAOM

NAOMI

*The Rise and Rise of the
Girl from Nowhere*

LESLEY-ANN JONES

VERMILION
London

To

Mia Clementine Jones

First published 1993

1 3 5 7 9 10 8 6 4 2

First published in the United Kingdom in 1993 by Vermilion
an imprint of Ebury Press
Random House UK Ltd, 20 Vauxhall Bridge Road, London SW1V 2SA

Random House Australia (Pty) Limited
20 Alfred Street, Milsons Point, Sydney
New South Wales 2061, Australia

Random House New Zealand Limited
18 Poland Road, Glenfield
Auckland 10, New Zealand

Random House South Africa (Pty) Limited
PO Box 337, Bergvlei, South Africa

Random House UK Limited Reg. No. 954009

A CIP catalogue record for this book is available
from the British Library

ISBN 0 09 178282 1

Typeset in Goudy by SX Composing Ltd, Rayleigh, Essex
Printed in England by Clays Ltd, St Ives plc

Contents

Thank You . . .

My sincere thanks to:

Naomi Campbell, for inspiring me to write about her.

Judy Chilcote, my Literary Agent and valued friend.

Rowena Webb, my Editor, whose encouragement, unflagging enthusiasm and tireless efforts shaped this book.

Keren Levy, who never takes no for an answer.

Sarah Bennie, a breath of fresh air.

Nick Gordon, for a dozen years of encouragement.

Tim Miles and David Williams, the most generous journalists on the Street.

Brian – who's got a lot of songs to sing.

The late Roger Scott – now dancing in the dark.

Joe Bangay, for an enlightening visit to Jamaica.

'Scoop', for 15 years of cherished friendship, who organised and cajoled me, spent countless hours transcribing interview tapes (yes, there *is* a God!) and in dusty libraries and archives all over London, who never once lost his rag and without whom this book would *not* have been possible.

Thanks also to:

Antonia Downey	Geoff the Chef
Roger Tavener	Chris Mitchell
Susan Blond	Chris and Ray Forster
Lowri Turner	David Syner
Todd Oldham	Lulu and Mike Appleton
Michael Watts	Henry Hecht
Louize Howard	Richard Johnson

Nadine Johnson
Cory
Anna Moana Pozzi
Liz Lawley for Falmer
    Clothing Company
Peter Stephenson-Wright for
    Lowe, Howard Spink
Terence Donovan
Berni Kilmartin
Tinu Majek
Pamela Clarke Keogh
Nick Elgar
Leigh Genis
Julie Hall
Sandy Evans
Vicki Woods
Jeannette Arnold
Sandy Williams
Jonathan Morrish
James Young

David Massey
Barbara Speake
June Collins
Julie Layton
Terry O'Neill
Loanna Morrison
Denise Lilley
Hal Austin
Paul Henderson
Linda Stein
Sylvia
Pat Puttnam
Carole White
Peter Sheridan
Sam Schwat
Chips Chipperfield
Hal Lifson
Joe Major
Pené

and all the other contacts in the fashion, media and entertainment industries, at Scotland Yard, the Home Office, the Inland Revenue and the FBI, who cannot be identified but whose contributions were invaluable.

Last, by no means least, my thanks and love to my father, the *Independent*'s Chief Sports Writer Ken Jones, without whose example and encouragement I would never have picked up a pen in the first place; who survived, last December, an horrific encounter with a British Rail train which claimed his right forearm but failed to smash his spirit, and who has since achieved more with one hand than most of us could ever manage with both.

Lesley-Ann Jones
September 1993

Where Do You Go To My Lovely . . .

It was The Story with Everything: illegitimate street-wise beauty plucked from the obscurity of South London's backstreets to be a fashion model, reinvents herself in New York, joins the multi-million-earning ranks of the Supermodels and captures the hearts of some of the world's most eligible men. One of those Must-Have exclusive interviews that colour magazines spend months and fortunes competing with each other to secure – and I happened to be the journalist assigned by *You* magazine to get it.

My interview with Naomi Campbell in New York in June 1992 was the result of endless approaches to her publicists, her agents, her American lawyer, and a wild-goose chase which had taken me from London to Manhattan to Los Angeles, back to London and on again to New York. Exasperated by Naomi's elusiveness, *You's* fearless former editor Nicholas Gordon finally despatched me to the States 'for as long as it takes' to interview everyone I could lay my hands on who either knew Naomi personally or had ever had professional dealings with her. From these, I would write a profile of the Supermodel to accompany the magnificent Herb Ritts photographs we had acquired.

The resultant piece was not entirely flattering, dealing as it did with a Scarlet Pimpernel of the catwalk whom everyone was talking about, but about whom little was really known. It was typical of the way Naomi does things that the minute my copy was filed she granted the magazine an interview, thanks to the persistence of commissioning editor Sandy Williams. Thus I found myself on a Kennedy-bound plane within twenty-four hours of landing in

London from Los Angeles, after an exhausting three-week stint on her trail.

It was an eye-opener of a breakfast: Naomi arrived with her new publicist Susan Blond, a one-time Warhol-ette. I had been smelling sour grapes for months, and I was prepared to dislike the Super-model whose reputation went before her: a moody, self-centred, attention-seeking bitchy one at that. But she knocked the wind from my sails. She was sweet and charming and funny, she patiently answered my questions, she did not shy away from taboo subjects like illegitimacy, famous boyfriends, and cattiness on and off the catwalk. She handled the interview like a pro. She did herself proud, and everyone was happy with the result.

When it came to researching this book, however, it was a different story. Far from being co-operative, Naomi and those close to her did everything to stand in my way. One door would close, another would slam in my face. Contacts clammed up, and I experienced problems every time I approached someone new. A magazine feature was one thing, reasoned Naomi's aides on her behalf, but a book was a blatant intrusion. Susan Blond, the consummate professional, tried to help me and lost Naomi as a client. Her replacement and I started out on the wrong foot, and communication between us was short-lived.

All this increasing hostility indicated that there must be something I was not supposed to find out. I had planned to write a straightforward book in praise of a humble Streatham girl who had conquered the international jet-set by her own efforts, whom I actually liked and admired – and I had, it seemed, though quite unwittingly, opened up a can of worms.

Undeterred, I began to research in earnest, interviewing dozens of contacts both here and in the United States, and attempting several more times to speak to Naomi and her mother Valerie. The reaction was not a friendly one.

I could not blame Naomi, her mother or their various friends and colleagues for not wishing to cooperate with me. That is their choice, and indeed their right. But where Naomi, her family and others close to her had backed out of the frame, others were swift to leap in. There were obviously skeletons in the cupboard, and they were beginning to rattle pretty loudly.

By now, for me, there was no turning back. Sure, the Naomi Campbell story had been told superficially in journalism and in girls' pamphlets many times before. But it had never been researched in every aspect. She fascinated me in a way no subject had done for a long time. What was her magic, what were her secrets? Where does she go to, this beautiful creature, when she's alone in her bed? Not since Twiggy in the 1960s had an ordinary young girl with a nice face made such an impression on the world simply by smiling for the camera, by putting on and taking off clothes. I was compelled to seek the real Naomi, to separate the wheat from the chaff, the true from the false, the real character from the larger-than-life legend. To write the first full-length, in-depth biography of the most spectacular Supermodel in the business; the London-born star of a truly American saga of success.

1

Legend

N*aomi Campbell* sits as still as a waxwork before a vast, illumi-
nated mirror while the make-up man goes to work on her face.
Taking colours mixed on the back of his hand with a fine sable
brush, he dabs and blends, smooths and strokes and polishes to perfection the famous Campbell features, as recognizable to most
women as their own. He is assiduous, respectful, almost reverential
in his approach. He works as deftly and as silently as a mime artist,
neither inviting nor expecting conversation from the ebony icon.
She, in turn, gives nothing as she glares dispassionately at what
appears to be her own reflection. She has seen it all before.

Around the calm couple, all hell is breaking loose. Opposite a 15-
foot-wide open window bearing a sign saying 'Do Not Close',
Roseanne Barr is doing God knows what to Naomi's personal rack,
where all her outfits hang wrapped in plastic with little Polaroids on
them showing how the accessories should go. Seven of the make-up
artist's assistants are slopping Chanel moisturizer with gay abandon
and cussing each other out of the way. The atmosphere is *wild* –
there are photographers and models all pushing and shoving each
other every which way, they can barely hear themselves think. The
models are skittish and edgy – you only have to walk past them and
they flinch. Everywhere you look there is make-up and food and
clothes . . . and *wigs*. Lined up on a trestle table close by, the hair-
pieces look like nothing so much as a bunch of little dogs. . . .

Clutching their coveted invitations, the Frockocracy dash down
Fifth Avenue in the rain towards the New York Public Library at
42nd Street, a regular fashion venue. They come in whooshing
limousines, in bouncy yellow taxis or on foot beneath vast golf

umbrellas. They come in black bell-bottoms, white ruffled blouses and platform pumps, all wearing the same lipstick and looking like a bunch of crows – one magazine's accessory editor stands out in the throng only because she is weighed down by fifteen crucifixes. And they come to be dazzled, or to pretend to be, by someone's interpretation of what next season's Look should be all about.

Editors and buyers stand around impatiently, sneaking last-minute cigarettes. There are a lot of women – the few men present are all acting like women – and you could cut the attitude here with a knife. They don't want to wait in a line, they want their tickets *now* – the atmosphere is charged. Tonight they get ushers and seats, but later in the week they will attend shows where they will have to fight their way in. New York Fashion Week is like a series of back-to-back movie premieres. Come Friday you will have seen the same cast of people all week, and will know everyone there is to know.

Inside the Library's Celeste Bartos Forum, a large room heaving with razzle-dazzle, the music is so loud that you can't even hear the applause. Then suddenly you can. It crashes towards the gleaming black Supermodel all the way from the back of the room: a relentless crescendo, deafening in volume, which all but cancels out the throbbing rock music to which she struts. Tonight's *pièce de résistance* is the ultimate in little yellow numbers, an eye-catching creation worked in satin and silk. The lung-tight, strapless yellow bodice is belted so severely at the waist it looks set to slice the model clean in two. A short but chic black jacket dripping in multicoloured appliqué blossoms slides alluringly from a perfect shoulder as she shoots a familiar 'Screw you' glare at photographers. A pair of outsized, sun-shaped gilt orbs dangle from her lobes like Christmas tree decorations. The red, red lips are pursed in delicious defiance. And the *legs*! . . . You have never seen legs like them. They go on and on forever. . . .

It is not this outrageously glamorous outfit which inspires such thunderous appreciation. It is *her*. Still Naomi sashays to and fro, a mesmerizing vision in the platinum spotlight. Then, for a split second, her enigmatic Gioconda smile breaks into full beam – and she disappears from the catwalk.

Backstage, smiling and relaxed, she patiently sheds yet another ludicrously expensive creation with the help of her dresser, who attacks rows of buttons, fiddles with fastenings, retrieves the last-minute pins. Naomi kicks off her spindle-heeled pumps with an oath and a sigh, flops into a chair, and sets about massaging the aches out of the feet she loathes more than anything: 'They're much too big! Just look at them!' She swigs Coke from a can, stuffs chocolates into her mouth three at a time from a ribboned box – the only thing she says she has had time to eat all day – and sloshes make-up solvent over her face which she cleans off with cotton wool before wiping her hands on a lipstick-stained towel.

There is a cardboard sign backstage which says: 'Don't even THINK about smoking!' Of course, all the models are smoking like mad. Five camera crews are waiting impatiently to interview the beaming designer, the models are climbing back into the clothes they came in and tossing belongings into their bags. Things are sighing back to normality. To one side, a food table appears to have been attacked by a ruck of vultures . . . or a bevy of frantic models too rushed to look for the trash can. There are empty mineral bottles tossed everywhere; apples with one bite taken out of them, the munched green edges stained with cerise lipstick; the same gloss slicks with mouth shapes the rims of white plastic cups. It is also smeared on the discarded orange peel, the half-eaten cookies, the water crackers, even the odd bottle of Perrier Jouet champagne: you help yourself to a swig of one lurking in a Perspex ice bucket now filled with water. All around the make-up artists are stuffing the tricks of their trade into a variety of black make-up cases and plastic shopping bags. At the back, in a curtained-off changing area, a long pale leg emerges through the black drapes as a model attempts to retrieve her escaping knickers with her big toe. . . .

Out front, about thirty straggling guests are left gossiping in the auditorium, now eerily quiet. An emaciated usher in black jeans and T-shirt marches up and down between the rows of gilt chairs snatching the name tags from the backs of seats: MTV, *Vanity Fair*, Saks Fifth Avenue, *New York Times*. And a little girl in a frothy pink dress, the daughter of one of the models, is running up and down the catwalk all by herself.

It is now almost 8 p.m., and what Naomi longs for most is her bed. Yet her head will not hit the pillow for at least another three hours. The Collections are nothing if not all go. Raking her hair with elegant fingers, she wriggles into a floral chiffon dress, yanks on a navy Chanel jacket, grabs her Chanel tote bag and makes for a side door, where a waiting limousine will whisk her into the damp New York night. . . .

You have observed her at close range for over two hours. And still you are none the wiser. Naomi Campbell, the world's greatest Supermodel, wafts in on a cloud of gossip and rumour, says little, dolls up, gives out on the catwalk big-time for half an hour – a nice little earner at between $10,000 and $25,000 a go – then retreats again from the spotlight to enjoy a morsel of private life before the whole procedure begins again. The other Supermodels can only stand and stare at the effect she has simply by walking into the room.

She is only twenty-three years old! And already she has earned more money, fielded more fame, been on more exotic dates than most of us could ever dream of in a lifetime. More has been written about Naomi Campbell since her rise and rise to glory than about all the other Supermodels put together. Her reported life story is a shifting melange of flimsy facts, erratic rumour, supposition and pure unsubstantiated invention, if such a thing can be called pure. There are few hooks to hang anything on, and neither she nor those around her have ever given very much away. Naomi has granted only a handful of proper interviews during her entire career, and has contradicted herself in most of those: as if to throw inquisitors off the scent in their quest to discover the real Naomi behind the sensational Supermodel.

But even the world's most glamorous profession has its downside. Being Naomi Campbell cannot be as easy as it looks.

'When they're up there on the catwalk you look at them and think: "How *wonderful* to be that beautiful, how magical life would be,"' admits the London *Evening Standard*'s fashion writer Lowri Turner, who spends a sizeable proportion of her working life watching models flaunt their most valuable assets along the catwalks of New York, London, Paris and Milan.

'Then you see them after the show coming out of the side door. You see these *things* – and they *are* things – they're just strange creatures who look completely bizarre when you put them next to normal, ordinary-looking people. When the make-up has been wiped off, they've shed the wigs and they're back in their everyday clothes, and they're just walking about the place, not performing, they are giant and skinny and weird-looking, like they dropped in from another planet.'

Fairytale lifestyle is what the glamorous world of modelling is supposed to be all about – but things are not always what they seem. Nobody would expect gorgeous Flavour of the Decade models to be really lonely girls. Girls whose relationships don't work because they are endlessly on the move. Girls who are obliged to go out to dinner with clients night after night, and then eat hardly anything at all, because that is what the clients expect. Girls who then go back to their hotel rooms at midnight and down a bottle of vodka and scoff six Mars bars. Have-it-all girls who have a desperate air about them, as if they are striving to stay on top all the time, to get the next job, and the next one, then the next . . . and once you're a *Super*model it is even worse, because you've got to keep going higher and higher and there isn't any higher to go. . . .

Even the world's toughest gossip columnists will acknowledge that the Supermodel's lot is not always a happy one. Some of them even sympathise. In an East 42nd Street bar near Manhattan's

Grand Central rail terminal, one gossip writer who has filled count-less column inches with revelations about Naomi's life and times still has plenty to say about the British girl who knocked New York for six.

'Quite the little household name, your Naomi, isn't she?' remarks distinguished columnist Richard Johnson, then of the *New York Daily News*, now back at the more illustrious Page Six on the *New York Post*.

'But I'll bet she's pretty insecure about it. It's a hot seat at such a young age. There *are* black American girls as beautiful as Naomi, of course. Though I think she *is* pretty beautiful, there might be some black American girls who are *as* gorgeous. What many people can-not understand is why this black English girl has made it so big here when this is where we *breed* black models. But it is generally agreed that she has the best legs in the business. Must be all those years of ballet. I don't know that she's the sharpest person on the planet, mind you. Johnny Casablancas, who owns the Elite model agency which represents Naomi, had a modelling talent show at the Plaza Hotel a couple of winters back. Naomi was the MC. The thing was really badly produced, no rehearsals, and Naomi was ridiculous! There were all these European models with unpronounceable names, and Naomi was supposed to announce them. She screwed up like there was no tomorrow. In the end, Casablancas turned to her at the microphone and said something like "Well, Naomi, don't you have to go and change now?!" Yet I have to say, she did look fabulous – in this terrific lace catsuit. The trouble is, they look that great, you can forgive them anything. . . .'

Forget actress or pop singer. The model-girl fantasy as epitomized by Naomi appears to be the most universal contemporary dream. It fires the imagination of young women from all walks of life: from waitresses and hostesses, supermarket checkout girls and barmaids, to college students, gels of independent means and even princesses. Forget talent, skill or any natural gifts involving singing, aero-nautical engineering or the speaking of foreign languages. By virtue of their beauty alone do they now have the chance to become one of the world's most adored females. Only a handful will make it to the top – incredibly, there are just 450 full-time fashion models in the whole of the United States – and precious few of those will make it big-time. Even more significant is that perhaps only eight or nine models in the world could legitimately call themselves Super-models. And part of the reason that they are so super is that there are so few of them.

So what does it take to be, like Naomi, a Supermodel? And where did the notion of Supermodels actually spring from? Arguments rage as to who are the main players – the real hard-core Supermodels – and the media attention focused upon them puts the Julia Robertses and Madonnas well in the shade. Perhaps one reason why the Supermodels have superseded traditional stars of stage and screen is that they have retained an aura of glamour in an age obsessed with warts-and-all realism. Today's movie stars tend to play it down in old sweaters and blue jeans, and spend their time campaigning to save whales and rainforests rather than putting on the glitz and hanging out in nightclubs. You will rarely if ever see a Supermodel in her curlers or looking less than her gorgeous self. She is always perfectly coiffed and styled, manicured and made-up. She's in with the In-Crowd, and wherever it's happening, she's already there.

'These are the new glamour queens all over the world', said one fashion editor. 'Modelling has become the new Hollywood.' Super-model is the new Mute Movie Star, Miss Perfect Seen-and-Not-Heard. It doesn't actually make much difference what she says or how she says it: she is sometimes known to let herself down merely by opening her mouth. She shouldn't fret: she is hired to be a walkie, not a talkie. Witty backchat is not part of the Supermodel's brief. It is something that Naomi and her catwalk sisters are always getting annoyed about, but they shouldn't do: the biggest bucks are paid for what amounts to the Silence of the Glams. This is the same theory that consigns women to one of two categories: beauty without brains, or brains without beauty. Good Lord, but we are not allowed to have both!

Supermodels are everywhere. *Harpers and Queen, Vogue, Elle,* features, advertisements, gossip columns, television commercials, street hoardings and chat shows, selling everything from Chanel jackets to perfume to cars to ice cream. And when the fashion shows kick off in spring and autumn in Paris, Milan and New York, you'll see them decked out in exotic creations on the tabloid front pages every day. They are beautiful, sexy, powerful, at least as famous as their boyfriends, and as high-profile as the couturiers whose clothes they flog. They have first refusal on all the major assignments, the best magazine covers, the fashion shoots, and they earn unbelievable money. For Supermodelling is nothing if not about dosh. Their contracts started to get so huge for the simple reason that, in a worldwide recession, they could still inspire consumers to part with hard-earned cash. What's more, they are a proven commodity all over the world, not just in the USA and Europe. Those same faces and figures sell scent and denims in Melbourne, Rio and Seoul. And the same few girls continue to claim the cream of the contracts because they are a safe bet. Few clients are prepared to take a risk on an unknown quantity when they are guaranteed success with a known one.

Supermodelling is, however, a relatively new domain. It was not until the 1970s, when fashion became a full-blown global industry, that its advertising expanded into the mass market and models were suddenly in demand in many territories at once. Today, they hop from one international location to another in a way that was unheard of twenty years ago. But the capital of the modelling industry remains New York, and that is why most of the Supermodels are based there.

Another factor which brought about the Supermodel syndrome was the cross-over by certain models between editorial and catwalk assignments. Where once it was a case of never the twain shall meet, the same models are now frequently employed by both maga-zine editors and fashion designers. In the good old days, designers rarely used models other than their own in-house mannequins to display their clothes. It was Kenzo, in 1970, who first used models from the fashion spreads in his Paris Collections, partly because one of his publicists had worked with some of them. The practice did not become commonplace until the end of the seventies. Today, it is unusual for a big-name designer *not* to use them, and indeed he is making a negative statement about his own status if he does not.

'In certain shows', reported one photographer, 'if Linda, Christy or Naomi is not coming down the runway, then no one looks.'

It was in January 1990 that British *Vogue* featured on its black, white and pink front cover a tantalizing line-up of five of the world's most sought-after fashion models: Cindy Crawford, Christy Tur-lington, Linda Evangelista, Tatjana Patitz and the only British, the only *black*, girl: Naomi Campbell. Among the thousands who admired the stunning cover shot was multi-millionaire pop singer George Michael. He was inspired then and there to try and cast the very same models, all together, in the ridiculously expensive pop video for his next single, 'Freedom'. Not only was it no mean logis-tical feat – the Famous Five were rarely in the same country at the same time – but it was also a controversial decision, not least because the singer himself was refusing to appear in his own video, in those days an unprecedented move. And not only that, but Michael, by now at odds with the music industry and the way it ex-ploits imagery to sell records, was in fact using these models to make a political point.

'I decided I'd had enough of it all,' he said candidly. 'I got sick of the visual image of a pop star being the most important thing – more important, in fact, than the music: the triumph of style over con-tent. By selling myself so hard through the eighties I found I was left with a desire to see how much I could do without it. I am also sick of the way pop stars hijack the sexuality of others and use it to promote their own ends. In this video I wanted to do exactly what I was objecting to, and in the most extreme form possible. It was time to make a statement.'

Michael was not kidding. Employing a team of sixty, including acclaimed director David Fincher, he hired the services of *Vogue*'s finest cover girls to lip-synch (none too convincingly) to the words of his new song. Christy Turlington was then twenty-one, a New Yorker who had been contracted by designer Calvin Klein at the age of nineteen for $1 million. Linda Evangelista, recently bleached, was then twenty-five, still married, and resident in New York and Paris. Tatjana Patitz was a twenty-three-year-old German living in New York. Cindy Crawford, the same age, wife-to-be of actor Richard Gere, was hostess of her own MTV show and had homes in New York and Los Angeles. And Naomi Campbell, then twenty, was living in New York, had finished with Mike Tyson and was now dating Robert De Niro. All were millionairesses who had surged to the top on account of their reflections. The age of the Supermodel had reached its zenith almost as soon as it had begun. Beautiful girls had always appeared in rock stars' videos: a prime example was Christie Brinkley in her husband Billy Joel's 'Uptown Girl'. Now they were doing it for serious money. Even George Michael had to come down from his politically correct podium for a second to admit:

'They all looked like they were from another planet. They are amazing. Christy Turlington is the most perfect-looking person I have ever seen. Her body looks like somebody just *drew* her.' A syndrome was born. And whatever the Vauxhall car manufacturers set out to do three years later for their Corsa commercials, it could never have had the same impact as George Michael's video shock tactics. It had already been done.

As much as he had mercilessly poked fun at what the Supermodel amounts to – nothing more than what he deemed the 'triumph of style over content' – Michael had done these five girls the ultimate favour by raising their asking price beyond all reasonable clout. Just after the single was released in autumn 1990, Italian designer

Gianni Versace hired the same models to mime to Michael's single on the catwalk at the opening of his flamboyant Milan show. It blew the fashion world's collective mind.

Said Lowri Turner, who was there to witness it live, 'That was when we all realized this was no longer about clothes – it was about *them*, the models. They had become far more important than even the Collections. It was an unbelievable turnaround. That was the apotheosis of the Supermodels.'

Since then, women's magazines have done much to enhance the Supermodel's role as an icon for nineties' women. And they are so widely read as to be far more culturally significant than any heavy-weight feminist tome. *Cosmopolitan*, for example, is published in no fewer than seventeen countries and imported into countless others. Having recently adopted an aspirational, I-can-do-anything stance, with the emphasis on personal image and sexual relation-ships, the Supermodel is nothing if not their perfect role model, the very embodiment of the attitude. Furthermore, the space between advertising and editorial is today so narrow as to be virtually insig-nificant. Whether the Supermodel is appearing in one, or the other, or even both, there is little difference: all eyes are still on her.

Three decades after the heyday of the malnourished-looking Twiggy, the ultimate Supermodel reigns in stark contrast to her wan predecessor. Naomi Campbell's portrayal of Modern Woman is statuesque, strong, totally in control and impossible to ignore, with an expression veering between the confidently alluring and the icy, standoffish stare. She is nothing if not a fairytale princess for grown-ups.

As to why modern women need Supermodels, American femi-nist Camille Paglia has no doubts. Contrary to being what many critics denounce as 'the final blow to feminism', Paglia says they have a vital role to play.

'The nineties' cult of Supermodels is a revival of the great system of Hollywood stars, which I totally applaud. I've never regarded Hollywood glamour as superficial – it is an art form. We're in a period now where actresses like Meryl Streep and Michelle Pfeiffer are more serious and go against glamour . . . so there's a vacuum which we have been in for fifteen years, and now the Supermodels are really beginning to satisfy this international need for hyper-glamour. Who wants to go to the movies and see women who are not interested in glamour? Because of this they can't pull in the same audiences as men. It is the men who have retained their mas-culine glamour, and who therefore are worth bigger salaries. It's a fact: we would rather look at Linda Evangelista because of her glamour, and that is why she is paid so much more than Meryl Streep.'

Possibly. By turning her beauty into a lucrative career, a woman may have achieved sexual equality in one way – but only for herself. She is in fact still letting the side down by continuing to conform to a male ideal. However, she is to be admired if only for the fact that she has learned how to exploit herself rather than be exploited by others.

Paglia goes on to point out that the Supermodels are the natural heirs of Dietrich and Garbo. And not only that: 'Modelling is in fact an art form with graceful gestures equal to the beauty of fine statues – in effect, fashion is artwork for the masses. The Super-model has made the transition into what films used to provide. The French know very well that fashion is an art form, but in Britain and America there is this dreadful Anglo-Saxon, puritanical attitude that Supermodels are trivial and superficial.'

But she insists that these are still early days in the equality battle. 'At this point in the nineties, women are still trying to figure out how to be sexual and be career women at the same time. The Super-models have an important role in breaking down barriers because their image is such a powerful one. There's no avoiding our need for what they provide: they are Icon and Role Model at once. They earn every penny.'

The syndrome would appear to have come full circle. According to Lowri Turner, the composite definition of a Supermodel is that

she crosses over between designers and styles and is used by everybody. 'She is extremely versatile,' says Turner. 'Not only can she do
all the shows, but for a designer *not* to have her is a statement: "I'm
too poor to afford this or that girl." It's lessening now, partly
because many people can't actually afford them – they command
such high fees, but partly because designers are getting tired of
having to shell out so much money. Thus, the girls are off doing car
ads and things. They are not necessarily available any more.'

The five top Supermodels having retained their status, Naomi remains the most visible of them all. And everybody in the business
has a theory about what makes her special.

'She was the first black girl to make a real impact', says *Harpers
and Queen* editor Vicki Woods. 'It was a combination of Anna
Wintour arriving at American *Vogue*, and putting Naomi on the
cover. Plus Naomi was then at the height of her beauty, she was a
dancer, she was able to move, she was the right size. The Supermodel syndrome was at that stage very new. The media had only
just decided to focus on them, and it was all to do with timing. If you
start hyping people, styling them, writing about them all the time,
you've got a very successful package. That was the major motivation of the late eighties, and Naomi really came in on the tail-end of
that bandwagon. The fact that she was black, frankly, made her
stand out.'

Naomi's visibility, according to American writer Michael
Musto, was the key factor. Suddenly, he says, 'She was everywhere.
Everywhere. The typical American woman probably feels as if she
knows Naomi Campbell's features better than her own. Her face
peers out from magazines, video screens and billboards wherever
you look. She has become an icon of the moment.'

For Lowri Turner, the walk has it: '*Nobody* can walk the catwalk
like Naomi. Most girls are good, but Naomi is unbelievable. She
bends her body in directions it was never meant to go. She has the
most beautiful, most perfect angles, not to mention ankles! Nobody

can take her place on the catwalk. It is partly confidence; if you're walking in massive high heels, you've got to have a lot of confidence to lean right over. And it's practice. She's been around, she's a real pro. Beyond that, it's a fact that black girls always walk better than white girls. Naomi may fall down occasionally, but she doesn't look as if she's worried about it.'

Monique Pillard, President of Elite New York, says Naomi is likely to stay the world's top Supermodel for some time. 'She is the greatest mover in the business. She oozes sex appeal and really knows how to work the body.' What's more, says the small but significant Pillard, Naomi is not too big-headed to play the game. 'There is a lot of pressure. She is still very young, and is asked to behave in a very adult way. Most of the time, she copes admirably.'

Society photographer Terry O'Neill says: 'On the catwalk, Naomi is Queen. I sometimes get the impression that she is not all that confident when posing for pictures, but she overcomes that with her sense of humour, which models don't often have. I usually need to direct her a little, but she's a remarkable girl. She's a one-woman show. You can't help looking at her – she has endless energy, and she always looks in control. She has a great presence. You sometimes have to remind yourself how young she is. For an English girl she is extraordinary. Most of them can't pose to save their lives. It's not in their nature, but it is in hers. It is a kind of magic, and you either have it or you don't. You can't learn it. I can remember a time when we, the photographers, were the big stars. Bailey, Donovan. . . . Not any more. Then it was the clothes, now it's the Supermodels, and Naomi is the best of the bunch.'

Much of Naomi's success is linked to the fact that she is one of just a handful of black girls in a business dominated by blondes leading the blondes. For black is still not the norm. The rag trade, perhaps, could use a little scrutiny when it comes to race relations. In 1991 a study by the US Department of Consumer Affairs found that American and Asian models are still blatantly discriminated against. The study, which examined 157 fashion catalogues and more than 11,000 print ads, discovered that while 12 per cent of magazine readers are African-American, blacks account for only 3 per cent of the models in the ads, and less than 5 per cent in catalogues. The figure shrinks to a lean 1 per cent for Asians. Most of the minority models featured were depicted in one of only four roles: musician, athlete, celebrity or object of pity. The problem, of course, isn't limited to advertising. Editorial representation of ethnic minorities has traditionally been poor.

February is the poorest month in the advertising sales calendar. It is also invariably the month when black models find their way on to fashion covers. Says Revlon's first black cover girl Veronica Webb: 'They say, "Oops, it's February, gotta get our black girl." Even when we were highly desirable, there was still little work for us in comparison with white girls. When I first arrived in Paris, the hot tip was to tell anyone considering you for work tales of mothers and fathers from far-flung corners of the globe. As a black American, and the generational progeny of slavery with more blood lines than can be accounted for, I fitted the bill.'

Bethann Hardison, a model in the sixties and seventies who went on to design swimwear and produce fashion shows, runs her own New York model agency as well as the activist group Black Girls' Coalition, which she co-founded with David Bowie's model wife Iman to raise the public awareness on subjects ranging from homelessness to racism in advertising. Bethann also acted as a mother figure to Naomi when she first arrived in New York, and often accompanied her to church in Harlem. She says: 'The role of the black model was stimulated in the early seventies by the slogan "Black Is Beautiful". Roughly ten years ago another ground swell occurred, with support from magazines such as *Elle* and British *Vogue* helping to make stars out of black models Karen Alexander and Gail O'Neil. The trend culminated in the rise of Naomi Campbell, who has come to symbolize *the* black model for her generation.'

But for the rest, especially among the ranks of photographers, make-up artists and stylists, not to mention the models, the disparity between black and white is still marked. 'Nine times out of ten on a shoot', says Naomi's nineteen-year-old catwalk rival Tyra Banks, 'I'm the only black person. Sometimes I don't even realize it until I get home.' It wasn't always so: in the eighties, during Black Is Beautiful's heyday, black models were so popular that *Women's Wear Daily* sniped: 'The runways of Paris are beginning to look like 125th Street.' Recalls Peggy Dillard, who posed eight times for the cover of *Vogue*: 'That wiped out black models for the next year.'

From the current designers' viewpoint, only a sprinkling of black models are listed among the must-haves: Veronica Webb, the overtly African-looking Roshumba Williams, Tyra Banks, and the newly shorn and now unashamedly ethnic Naomi Campbell – whom Banks was widely rumoured to have replaced.

'Ever since Tyra came on the scene, people have been working this "Baby Naomi" thing,' says an Elite model booker. 'You know, like Naomi's supposed to pack it in at twenty-two.'

'I don't know why,' says Tyra Banks. 'But people continue to act like there's only room for one black girl at the top.'

The sad reality is that this is indeed the case. So Naomi's triumph is two-fold. Not only is she the only British Supermodel, she is the only black one. And part of the reason that she is so much more visible than her predecessors is that we are in an age when models, not photographers or designers, call the shots. Last year, Claudia Schiffer signed a four-year deal with Revlon worth $6 million. Christy Turlington negotiated a non-exclusive contract with Maybelline for $2 million. Naomi still does not snare the same volume of advertising contracts as her blonde, blue-eyed sisters, nor has she yet been offered a deal by a major cosmetics company: when Revlon launched its first all-black range, the contract was awarded to lesser-known black model Veronica Webb. 'I may be considered one of the top models in the world,' remarked Naomi, 'but in no way do I make the same money as them.'

Still, she has a much higher profile – and has since admitted that she probably makes the money 'in kind'. And she, Linda, Cindy and Christy can expect to rake in up to $25,000 a day for catwalk

work at fashion shows. Naomi's personal fortune is currently estimated at well over £1 million. It is this sort of wealth which has
brought about the afore-mentioned shift in power between the professionals. As one top fashion photographer remarked, 'It's gotten
to the point where models control everything. Except for working
the camera, *they* are the ones taking the pictures.' Adds legendary
fashion photographer Richard Avedon: 'The money that top
models make now absolutely changes the relationship.'

Why? The basic allure of beauty is one thing, but there must be
more to it than that. It is as if they possess a special ingredient, a
quality which is as unexplainable as it is undeniable. A magic that
ignites the lens and transfixes the eye: something akin to 'presence'
in an actor. 'It's instantaneous. You *feel* it when you see it,' said
Elite's Gerald Marie.

The less we can keep our eyes off them, the more the Supermodels are worth. Yet it still doesn't explain why Naomi Campbell
is the most compelling of them all. Of more than a hundred people I
interviewed in New York about her, few were able to offer lucid ex-
planations. Take this one from Russell Simmons, owner of DEF
JAM Records, a prominent black record and TV producer, friend of
the stars and ultimate pitchman – he could, apparently, take a book
of matches and make people think it would light the world. . . .

'The reason Naomi is a star is that she's a very beautiful model, a
great model, she's very photogenic and has all the attitude in the
world. She's very personable, she has a lot of very supportive
friends, but even those qualities are secondary to what she's really
about. You know, she aggravates some people and they say she's
fucked up or whatever, but no matter what anybody says, all eyes
are still on her. That's a star. She's so talented, she has such personality, she could piss people off as much as she wants and they'd love
her all the more. Everybody *tomorrow* could stop loving her the way
we do, but she'd still be a star. Because she's got all that talent, the
designers recognize it, the photographers recognize it, *every* shot of
her looks good, so she makes all of *them* look good. It does no harm

doing business with her, baby. . . . What's she like *off* the runway? Man, she's one of the most fun people in the world! Going out with Naomi is like hanging out with a roller-coaster. Let's go here, let's go there . . . that woman will give you a heart attack!'

A top make-up artist defined her magic thus: 'She has so many different backgrounds in her face. She can look African, Jamaican, Chinese, Hispanic, Italian – that's very modern, very nineties, very *now*. The Berlin Wall is down, we got Bush out of office, now is the time for people to accept diversity – and Naomi is the ultimate representation of that. Everyone can relate to her in some way, even if it's in a bad way! In other ways she is so incredibly beautiful, it's scary. But she's also approachable – that's why people think she's so beautiful. She is friendly and bright and funny . . . and there's something behind the eyes. If a girl doesn't have that, it doesn't matter how beautiful their bone structure is. Cindy Crawford is one thing, but she pales into insignificance beside Naomi.'

Young New York designer Marc Jacobs, who made his name with Perry Ellis before launching his own fashion collection, believes her appeal has much to do with the way she moves. 'She's a dancer . . . she just dances down the runway. She's beautiful, she's got star quality.'

And American *Vogue*'s revered black creative director André Leon Talley puts it down to attitude: 'She has a lot of it. *A lot*. She has had to be very calculating and very ambitious. Some people say Tyra Banks does Naomi Campbell better than Naomi, but I wouldn't say she was a Supermodel. Naomi just pushes it to the limit, she dares, she gives it her all. It's all about performance and drawing the audience to you and what you are wearing. Attitude. Charisma. Presence. She's simply the best.'

Another fashion editor told me: 'She's just a genius in front of the camera. She knows what to do with her face and body all the time. It's really a gift. It's not something you can learn. I worked with Naomi when she just started – I took her down to the Hamptons for some outdoor stuff. She was shy then, but still great. Now that she has all this attitude there's no stopping her. She gets better and better – she's energetic and exciting. You get on a shoot with Naomi and you'll do *anything* for her, because she will do anything for *you*.'

Even her bad ratings are good. When I sat next to hot-shot designer Todd Oldham at a birthday party for designer Carolina Herrera's publicist, upstairs at the models' favourite and highly exclusive hang-out, Café Tabac, he told me: 'I won't use her. We have a No-Assholes clause.' But at Oldham's splashy, Indian-flavoured New York show, everyone took one look at Tyra Banks as she entered the room hip-bones first to huge ovations, cooed 'Get *her*!' and then demanded: 'But where's Naomi?'

She is here, there and everywhere . . . even when she's not. . . .

It is because today, Naomi's name is synonymous with Supermodel: *the* glamorous superstar for the nineties. She has worked on every inch of herself, from her accent to her taste in champagne. She rarely steps out without a designer label on her back. She wears fur coats and real diamonds. Her name appears on the A-list of all the right parties, she dances chic-to-chic at every one of them, each of her boyfriends has been a megastar, and her some-time fiancé, U2's bassist Adam Clayton, is one of the richest rock guitarists in the world today. She has done all this in spite of her lowly, illegitimate birth, of being abandoned by her father and raised by her hard-working single mother on South London's drab backstreets. She has done it despite the fact that she is black, which even in these apparently liberated times is no mean feat. She has done it without qualifications or family connections. All she had was her incredible beauty and a searing ambition to be the best. What else did she *need*?

It is one thing to admire her for her achievements – another thing entirely to sift the real Naomi from the glamorous image. The more you seek, the more you find that the only original thing about Naomi Campbell is her name. She has often been dubbed 'The

Streatham Stray Cat' – but where exactly did she come from? How did her Jamaican mother come to be living in London, and how did she support her daughter? These are the first in a string of questions to which only the vaguest answers have hitherto been known. It would also prove fascinating to learn how a child of such humble origins was able to attend two expensive London stage schools; what really happened that legendary afternoon in Covent Garden when Naomi is said to have been discovered by a modelling agent who launched her on a short, sharp journey to Happy Ever After; how the teenage Naomi came to begin a new life in New York – and *why*. And what was so special about her that set her apart from all the other top models, making her the fashion designers' ultimate favourite as well as object of desire to some of the world's most eligible men? What really happened the night she met the then Heavyweight Champion of the World, Mike Tyson, and what was it about her that so fascinated Robert De Niro, one of Hollywood's most enigmatic stars? What did Eddie Murphy offer to show her – and what did Viscount Linley ask her to show *him*? How did her affair with Sylvester Stallone come to light after it was all over, and what possessed her to become, even briefly, just another model on the arm of Eric Clapton? Who *is* Adam Clayton, one of the world's most anonymous millionaire rock stars – and how did he and Naomi meet and fall in love at the speed of sound?

There is clearly more to this girl than meets the eye. More than the media image which denounces her as a Superbrat who is loathed by the other Supermodels; who is said to be foul-mouthed, fickle, a bitch on and off the catwalk, an alleycat who slugs her girlfriends in the street and brawls in nightclubs; a Drama Queen who apparently throws tantrums at the drop of a hatpin, tosses herself like a rag doll at famous men, and threatens suicide if they won't come out to play. If she is all this (which she denies), why would the professionals put up with her? And if she isn't, then who is she really, and how do such malicious rumours spread?

Few people who have been alive less than a quarter of a century

At the Italia Conti School

At the beginning of her modelling
career, aged 15, with her mother at
home in Streatham

An early fashion
assignment for
British *Vogue* in
1988

Above: Behind the
scenes at the Paris
Shows

Dashing from show to
show during Paris
Fashion Week in 1989

Left: In New York with *Vogue*'s revered Creative Director André Leon Talley in 1989

Below: The *Vogue* cover picture for January 1990 that launched the Supermodel phenomenon

arouse so much unflagging interest, inspire so much passion, as Naomi. True, we tend to make special folk heroes of those at the pinnacle of their profession, particularly sportsmen and rock stars. But why a Supermodel? Do we really care, one way or another, about pretty girls who make millions not through any special talent but merely for exploiting their God-given assets? Does it blow our minds that Cindy Crawford is married to Richard Gere, or that Linda Evangelista has left her husband, model agency boss Gerald Marie, for *Twin Peaks* star Kyle MacLachlan? That Claudia Schiffer has had the odd date with Prince Albert of Monaco, or that George Michael thinks Christy Turlington has the perfect body? Not really. There are plenty who insist that all of these girls are better pros than Naomi, and for all we know they are right. Does it matter about Cindy and Linda and Christy and Claudia? Not much. Yet Naomi matters. As one news editor pointed out, 'I can't recall a day in the past three years when I did not hear the name Naomi Campbell in news conference.'

Almost every day, certainly every week, you either read or hear something about her. And along with the endless fascination with Naomi the Supermodel Icon, I found in those who know and work closely with her a surprisingly warm affection. Ask about Naomi and the first thing most people do is smile. They might have anecdotes to share which compound her Bad Girl image; they might even have crossed her in their time, and found themselves at the receiving end of her wrath. But the virtually invariable consensus was that Naomi is nothing if not value for money. Many were the references to her boundless energy and lively sense of humour, as well as to her generosity. In the words of one catwalk colleague, 'She'd give you the shirt off her back.' Presumably she wouldn't have had to pay for it. . . .

Many of the people I talked to were startlingly frank about some of the naughty things Naomi had done, the disastrous mistakes she had sometimes made. But through it all there was the warmth, a real delight. They clearly took pleasure in talking about her. She is, said most people, enormous fun to have around. They *like* her, they wish they saw her more. Perhaps the most telling aspect of her character was best articulated by her friend, model agency boss Bethann Hardison, when she said: 'As much as she gets out there with the stars, Naomi remembers what's important in life – and where she comes from.'

There was only one place to begin.

2

Many Rivers to Cross

Those colourful guide books which extol the virtues of Jamaica as
a chic, palm-fringed holiday destination make little more than
passing reference to its rich cultural mix. It was born of early Indian
and Spanish settlers, two centuries of shameful African slavery
during the heyday of the sugar and coffee plantocracy, predatory
pirates and buccaneers, the coming of East Indians, Chinese,
Cubans and endless others, and the eventual exodus of native
islanders in search of opportunities and a decent standard of living
they could no longer find at home. 'Out of many, one people' would
become Jamaica's official motto – and few other races boast such
strongly intermingled bloodlines.

Throughout the eighteenth century, thanks to the sugar trade,
Jamaica was Britain's most important colony. A hundred years later
it was falling into decline. By the mid-twentieth century the Caribbean story had in a bizarre way come full circle: the early pioneers
had seen in these islands the possibility of wealth, the certainty of
adventure; and today, their prosperous colonial lifestyle has been
recreated in all its hedonistic splendour for wealthy tourists who can
afford to spend their holidays there.

When the Second World War ended in 1945, Britain experienced rapid industrial growth which created a massive demand
for labour. But many British people were not prepared to work anti-
social hours for low pay in jobs that carried humble social status.
There was therefore such a severe shortage of labour in some industries that Britain was forced to turn to the 'Empire' for a cheap
source of workers.

Naomi Campbell's maternal grandfather, George James Morris,

was born in Jamaica on 1 October, 1923, and her grandmother, Ruby Moses Campbell, three years later on 9 March 1926. During her grandparents' youth, the island's population was expanding faster than its economy could keep up with it. Because most of the Caribbean islands depended on just one or two export crops, the Depression hit exceptionally hard. By 1933 crop prices had dropped by half, wages had fallen, taxes had risen and unemployment was running high. Most of the population existed below the breadline, lacking even the basics of housing, enough food and health care. The islands' own welfare programmes were inadequate. Extreme poverty had given rise to strikes and violence throughout the islands, which in turn brought about the formation of new unions and mass political parties. These achieved self-government, which eventually led to Jamaica becoming a fully independent member of the British Commonwealth in 1962.

During the 1950s, thousands of Jamaicans began to consider emigrating to Britain or the United States, both of which were experiencing an economic boom and where job prospects seemed more promising. Ruby and George were among them. Legally, it was easy for Jamaicans to emigrate to Britain, at least until the 1962 Immigration Act was passed. All you needed was money for your trip.

The majority of immigrants came on privately organized, independently funded packages, although some British corporations recruited West Indian labour locally. London Transport, regional health authorities, the British Transport Commission and a number of British hotel and restaurant chains were among those to launch recruitment drives in the Caribbean. By 1958 London Transport had some four thousand black workers, a quarter of them enlisted directly from the Caribbean.

For Ruby and George, and indeed for most of these hopeful immigrants, Britain was not the Land of Plenty they had envisaged. Discrimination was rife, and many trade unions barred the employment of blacks or at least imposed restrictions, fearful that black workers would bring down wages or even force their own members out of work. Protests were frequent, and it was not uncommon to find signs stating 'No Coloureds' on factory gates. Many immigrants also faced housing problems: long waiting lists, overcrowding, unscrupulous landlords turning a handsome profit on substandard accommodation. By 1961 there were 171,800 West Indians living in Britain, concentrated mainly in the inner city slums.

Perhaps the saddest aspect of all was the naivety which accompanied many emigrants' hope as they bade farewell to their beautiful islands and came looking for a better life. They had no idea how different, how cold, how fast, how *vast* Britain would be compared with home. One proud Jamaican, on disembarking at Folkestone Docks, was quoted as having enquired: 'Where can I get a taxi to Birmingham?'

A carpenter by trade, George Morris was thirty-four-years-old when he left Jamaica in March 1957 with Ruby Moses Campbell, then thirty-one, together with their young children June and Naomi's mother, Valerie Joan. Although Valerie was later to report that a third child, Delroy, also made the journey with them, her brother is not listed on the Immigration papers. Judging from the information given by Ruby on these papers, where she is identified by her maiden name Campbell, and by the fact that no certificate of marriage has come to light, it is reasonable to assume, though by no means certain, that the couple were not married. It is unlikely that Naomi's grandmother was a feminist who insisted on keeping her own surname; but it was, in those days, very common for illegitimate Jamaican children to take their father's surname. This would account for the fact that Valerie and her siblings were registered as Morris.

According to Valerie the family went first to Sheffield, where her father worked as a bus driver – like most Jamaicans who came to Britain at that time, he was employed below his skilled status – while Ruby joined the John Lewis department store group as a finisher. Immigrant families tended to stick together as clans and were very supportive of each other. 'We were a very traditional West Indian family, hard-working and very strict. I don't think I ever once argued with my mother,' remembered Valerie in a 1992 interview. Born on 4 December 1951, she had been five years old when her family came to Britain and could recall very little about the journey.

Shortly afterwards, when Valerie was six, they moved to 93 Flaxman Road, Camberwell, in South-east London. It wasn't poverty, but neither was it glitz. In those days racial harmony prevailed in that area of London, although later there would be ethnic tension. As Valerie explained: 'I integrated perfectly well with the other children.' It would be her lasting memory of her childhood.

When she was thirteen her family moved house within the Camberwell area, to 38 Paulet Road. As a teenager, Valerie grew tall and strong. She shone on the playing fields, and became known as something of a local beauty. As a sports lover she wanted to be an athlete, but the lure of showbusiness got the better of her and at the age of sixteen she became a dancer. 'I was always very ambitious,' she recalls, 'and I thought dancing was a way to reach the top, see the world and make money.'

For the next three years, she says, she had an extraordinary life, working in the Hilton in Athens, at casinos in San Remo, Beirut, Tehran and in Egypt, and appearing before Aristotle Onassis and the Shah of Iran. It seems to have been a hard life: 'We didn't get paid much, and we were fined for almost anything – for lateness, mistakes, or if there was a hole in our tights.'

So the story goes, she danced all over Europe and sent money home, a common enough practice among young black women of that era. But it was also a period in Valerie's life that remains something of a mystery. Although she often tells of her glamorous days cavorting with American dance troupes called Exotica and Fantastica, apparently once based in Rome, I, nor any other journalist have yet been able to trace any records of them or her co-dancers.

'That was a notorious dark spot in our history, young black girls going off to dance on the Continent from Britain in the 1960s,' says Hal Austin, a Barbadian-born news reporter on the *Daily Mail*. 'People just didn't talk about it. It would be "Haven't you just been to Germany – nudge-nudge – ?" I do not suggest that Valerie herself was involved in any kind of immoral activity. I am merely pointing out that, in many cases, the "dancing" element was a cover for something else.'

Valerie's period of working abroad certainly confounded the British tax inspectors, and her financial status made life difficult for her when she tried to re-establish herself in Britain in 1972. The Home Office actually considered turning down her application for re-entry at that time, their suspicions aroused by such matters as her passport, reported lost in August 1968 and reissued by the Jamaican High Commission in London. But because Valerie's records up until 1968 appeared to be in order, and because by this time she had a small child – Naomi – living in England with her own mother Ruby, she was granted permission for re-entry into Britain in 1972. Her papers indicate that she returned to live with a 'man friend'. But on the day of her interview, the official who saw her neglected to ask for this 'man friend's' name and details, so these are not recorded.

'Black girls were the thing in Europe at that time,' explains Loanna Morrison, glamorous showbiz columnist with Britain's biggest-selling black weekly, *The Voice*. 'A lot of them came from the West Indies, passed through New York and London and became exotic dancers in Europe. It was common. If you were beautiful and exotic-looking, you couldn't go wrong. Valerie had a large bosom, long legs and a very slim body – she had "the passport". A lot of wealthy European men in those days found black women extremely exciting, and would pay a lot of money just to sit and drink champagne with them after they danced. For many of them, that was enough. It seems very likely that a few of the girls would also engage in escort work – it was that kind of environment. But of course those activities would not have been openly discussed. Minimally educated, unqualified black girls had so few opportunities back then – they still don't – that if they had the body and the beauty they were stupid not to capitalize on that. It was their main asset – it was all they had.'

Loanna has first-hand knowledge of this kind of a lifestyle, since there are many parallels between her own upbringing and Naomi's. 'My own mother left home to work in another country and send money home. She used to wear bananas on her head, and dance on stage in a bikini,' Loanna admits. 'She left me behind in Jamaica in 1958 and went to New York to find a job. She had my sister, and met up with three or four other gorgeous black girls in New York. They formed a dance troupe, went to Europe and showed off their boobs. They'd heard you could get paid all this money just to dance on stage, then sit and drink champagne all night with ridiculously rich clients, so that is what they did.'

Her mother, she says, was suddenly 'quite well-off'. 'She worked in Milan and Rome, and in Lugano, Switzerland – you could do most of Europe and the Near East from Italy. She used to send all this stuff – polka dot waistcoats and trousers, bicycles, dolls – all the way from Milan for me. She'd send all these things by post to my grandmother in Kingston, who was looking after me, and maybe she'd come twice a year to see me. Now . . . how do you afford *that* if you're a nurse or a ward orderly – you know? Or a waitress. Or a bus conductress. You just don't. And you certainly couldn't afford an airline ticket, especially not in those days.

'And how do you meet a rich Italian who works as an accountant for an important banking firm, which she did, and marry him? Where do you meet him, hey? So she made all this money, she married him, she sent for me, and we lived in a penthouse apartment in Milan and had this very nice life. Later on I was sent to England to a posh boarding school – Rosemead in Littlehampton – and I would jet off home to Milan every holiday. My mother would never have got to meet such a man had she not danced and drunk champagne in the kind of places she worked in, and I wouldn't be at all surprised to learn that Valerie had done a similar thing.'

In 1969, when Valerie was eighteen, she fell pregnant by her current boyfriend in South London. 'I was dismayed,' she later recalled. 'It took all my courage to tell my parents, but they didn't throw me out and adoption was never considered. We are a black family which has always worked together, supported each other, taken every opportunity and achieved success.'

The Swinging Sixties flapped lamely to a close, and the first year of the new decade saw eleven-year-old Michael Jackson and his brothers, as the Jackson Five, hit the Top Ten four times with a series of hits: 'I Want You Back', 'ABC', 'The Love You Save', and 'I'll Be There'. It was the peak of their popularity in Britain. That was the year, that was, when Eric Clapton launched Derek and The Dominoes and released the eponymous album. When the Beatles kissed (or was it punched?) each other goodbye. When mini-skirts snapped out, midi-skirts drooped in, and the skinheads pummelled each other on the beaches. When Edward Heath and the Conservatives toppled Labour's valiant run under Harold Wilson, Palestinian terrorists were exploding jets in the Jordanian desert, and bloody combat raged in Cambodia and Vietnam.

On 22 May 1970, after a painful labour which lasted for three days, Valerie Morris gave birth to a baby girl at London's General Lying-In Hospital, York Road, Lambeth – an annexe of St Thomas's Hospital near Waterloo Station. It had been a brave decision for an unmarried black teenager living in a deprived part of South London to keep her baby, but abortion, for a girl from a religious family, was out of the question. Forty-two days later, on 2 July, she registered the child's birth herself at the London Borough of Lambeth Register Office. She had named her baby daughter Naomi Elaine Campbell, but gave her own name as Valerie Joanne Morris – 'A Dancer' – and her home address as 23 Kenwyn Road,

Lambeth. This was a rented room in a family house owned by a Jamaican couple, Alpheos and Sarah McKinson. The elderly and now widowed Mrs McKinson still owns the house and lives there to this day, but has no firm recollection of the unmarried black teen-ager and her baby.

There was no mention of the child's father on Naomi's birth certificate. In the spaces designated for his name and surname, place of birth and occupation, a line has been drawn through each.

The registration of a birth by a single mother is a fairly traumatic decision. This could be the reason why Valerie deliberated for almost six weeks before she could bring herself to go through with it. Perhaps she found it hard to decide whether she should record the father's name and relevant details. In such cases it is carefully explained to the mother by the Registrar that, once the birth certificate is completed and signed, the particulars on the original can never be changed. If a woman decides not to register the father's details, they may not be added at a later date to a new certificate without special authority from the Registrar General and the consent of the father, if the couple remain unmarried. In any case, the original would still be kept on record, although it would not be issued for general use. While such a decision will significantly affect a mother's chances if she later decides to seek maintenance from her child's father through the courts – it will be up to her and her counsel to prove paternity by a different method – it also reduces the father's chances of making any successful custodial claim, since it indicates that the mother alone assumes full responsibility for her child. While the presence of a name on a birth certificate does not prove that a man *is* actually a child's father, its absence is a fair indication that the mother wanted nothing more to do with him.

For this reason, it is a very serious decision to make. It can cause repercussions later in life if the child decides to go looking for the father, and asks questions as to why his or her father is not identified. Such a child may have problems coming to terms with what he or she often perceives as blatant rejection by a parent who would not stand up and be counted.

As for the child's surname on the birth certificate – Campbell – Valerie would later explain that she had, by this time, a stepfather called Alan Campbell, who gave the child his own name. 'My mother was upset because I was so young, but they stood by me,' said Valerie. 'As soon as Naomi was born, they took her on. That is why she's a Campbell – Campbell is my stepfather's surname.' By co-incidence, it is of course also her mother's maiden name – but then the name Campbell is as common in Jamaica as Jones is in Wales.

Her own father, it appears, had left Britain after his relationship with Valerie's mother Ruby ended, and went to start yet another new life in New York – where Valerie is said to have visited him as a child.

Twenty years later, in December 1990, Valerie had this to say about Naomi's real Dad: 'Naomi has no idea who her father is. I was four months pregnant and he was up and away. We never saw him again. He had mixed roots, with a bit of Chinese. He was very good-looking, but he wasn't someone who got up every morning and went to work. After he left, I blotted him out of my mind. And Naomi has blotted him out too.'

Shortly after Naomi's birth, Valerie left the baby with her mother and resumed her life as an exotic dancer. She was the bread-winner, and she says she had no choice. 'I left her behind', she said candidly in 1992, 'so that I could get on with my life. I think it is sad that most single girls today don't get that kind of family support. It was hard always being abroad, though. I missed my mother and sisters.' By this time there were step-siblings in her family, in-cluding a step-sister, Yvonne. 'But I had to send money back for the child. Naomi was accepted and loved. She settled down happily with the situation, and she saw me in the holidays.'

During my interview with Naomi in New York we discussed her illegitimacy, and how she felt about the father whom her mother had never named, and whom both mother and daughter insisted Naomi had never known. 'I think it has an effect on you before you are even born,' she told me. 'It affects your awareness . . . I think it makes you more sensitive.'

Naomi had obviously considered the possibility that her biological father might one day try to get in touch with her – and that she might even want to find him. But she had not yet made any firm decisions about how she would handle the situation. 'I don't know what I would do. I don't know,' she admitted. 'I wouldn't want to hurt my Mum or anything. I'm not ready yet, anyway. If I thought I might be ready to deal with it, maybe one day. And if my mother felt okay about it. But not now. I'm curious, of course. I'd like to find out all about him – in time. I think you have to be ready to face it. It's fundamental, it's in your heart. I'm sure there comes a time for all children when they have to find out.

'It is *always* going to hurt a single Mum who has brought up a child on her own. Then the kid wants to go off and look for the missing Dad! I watched a movie about that once, with James Cagney. They always go looking, kids, you know? But they come back! That's what you pray for.'

Of her mother's absences when she was little, Naomi was quite philosophical. 'She wasn't there too much during my childhood, it's true. But I can't be angry with her for that. She was working for *me*. People just don't understand, and I can't be bothered to explain. We didn't suffer as a result of our separation. We are very close today, and that's all that matters. Most people think we are like sisters. But she's still my Mum. We are very close, we talk about everything – I just can't swear in front of her! Actually I was never the kind of kid to sneak around behind my mother's back. If I wanted to tell her anything, shocking or not, I'd just come out with it. She prefers it that way. We are very open and straightforward, and she likes that.'

When Naomi was still a toddler, her mother says she took her daughter to live with her in Europe for a spell, but the arrangement did not work. 'I had her with me in Italy for a while when she was three,' said Valerie. 'But she started speaking too much Italian, so I got her back to England quickly.'

She had given up dancing by then and was trying to break into modelling. But there were few black models around in those days, and Valerie found it very difficult to get work. 'If you didn't have blonde hair and blue eyes you'd never get past the agency. I don't care about colour, but I told Naomi what I went through at that time to make her aware of prejudice. I said that nothing is impossible, but if you are black and want to be a success, you have to cope with a lot of heartache and rejection.'

Naomi celebrated her fifth birthday in May 1975, while she was staying at Flat 13 on the first floor of Hyperion House, a reasonably respectable block at the wrong end of Upper Tulse Hill, close to Brixton. She was enrolled at Holy Trinity Church of England School, just a short walk from her home, which she first attended the following September. According to her childhood snapshots she was a tiny child with a cute little heart-shaped face, enormous eyes and a cheeky grin – like so many others in the school playground. She wore her frizzy hair scraped back in a bow on top of her head, and tiny gold rings in her ears.

'Naomi Campbell was only here for the one term,' confirmed the school secretary at Holy Trinity. 'And nobody here now actually remembers her. She was at the school nearly twenty years ago, and our longest-serving member of staff has only been here for seventeen years.'

On 5 January 1976 her mother enrolled her at the Barbara Speake Stage School in West London. It was a considerable round trip each day to Acton and back again, but Naomi never complained.

During the next eight years she would move house twice more: first, with her grandmother and step-grandfather to Flat 66, Crowhurst House, Aytoun Road on the Stockwell Park Estate in London SW9 – not the kind of place one would expect to find a sophisticated showgirl from a European dance troupe. It was once the scene of an infamous sex crime involving a TV producer's daughter. The estate consists of yellow brick, three-storey, barrack-like blocks of flats. Today huge refuse bins shed their stinking contents on to humped roads dividing the crammed blocks, which are lined with badly parked second- and third-hand cars. On one corner, an abandoned mattress spills its guts and blocks access to the road. Religious graffiti is daubed on garage doors: 'FOR JESUS YOU GO AND REPENT'. A stench of refuse pervades the air, and the dank, sinister stairwells clearly double as urinals. Flat 66, Crowhurst House remains the home of Allan and Derek Campbell to this day.

Naomi's next home was in marked contrast to her previous run-down address. Number 83B, Drewstead Road in Streatham, London SW16 is an expensive-looking four-bedroomed house on a leafy avenue which dips down towards Tooting Common with its recreation ground, tennis courts, playground and outdoor swimming pool. The house, within walking distance of Streatham Hill mainline railway station, is a 1930s-built red-brick detached. The doors and window frames are, and were then, painted bright white with a smart navy blue trim. There are window shutters, security lights, a neat front garden, all the suburban trimmings. It is the nicest house on the street, and would probably fetch around £140,000 in the current climate.

It was this address which was given by both Naomi's mother Valerie and her husband-to-be, Clifford Blackwood, when they were married on 12 January 1982 at Lambeth Register Office. He was a twenty-nine-year-old bachelor, son of George Blackwood (an 'Engineer with London Transport'), and gave his own profession as 'Shop Proprietor – Food'. Valerie – still using her real surname, Morris, instead of changing it to what she often referred to as the 'family name', Campbell – gave her age as thirty, and indicated, with a line drawn through the space left for her profession, that she had now become a lady of leisure.

'At thirty I married Clifford Blackwood, who was a painter and decorator,' an interview stated in October 1992, thus contradicting some of the information on her marriage certificate. 'I gave up work and looked after Naomi, who was then eleven. My husband was hard-working and quite well-off, and an excellent stepfather to Naomi. She still talks to him on the phone. When we married he had less money than me, but you make compromises for love, and anyway all my money went on Naomi.'

Clifford George Alexander Blackwood was born in Kingston, Jamaica on 19 September 1952, and brought to Britain by his parents, George and Iris, when he was six years old. He grew into a tough but likeable young man who held his own on the streets of South London, and was known in several different manors – he changed addresses seven times between 1965 and 1976. Although these days he maintains a very low profile as the owner of a mini-cab firm in Brixton, and has a respectable home address in Purley, Surrey, he frequently operated on the wrong side of the law in his younger days. His criminal record lists nine previous convictions and several suspended sentences between 1975 and 1989, for a range of offences involving drugs and offensive weapons.

It seems likely that Valerie was aware of her husband's dark side – in October 1982, nine months after they were married, he was deported from Switzerland for being an illegal immigrant and an 'Undesirable'. In order to obtain a British visitor's passport he had impersonated his cousin, Carlton Blackwood. He had presented Carlton's National Health medical card at Stockwell post office as identification for the issue of the document, and gave his cousin's home address in Athlone Road, Tulse Hill, as his own. Clifford was then officially resident at Valerie's Drewstead Road, Streatham home, and his own passport was being held at Peckham police station. He claimed that he needed to travel to Switzerland because his wife, who was allegedly then in Geneva – her sister apparently owned a restaurant there – had fallen ill.

In the meantime Valerie returned to London and reported him missing. To the officer handling the enquiry she gave Clifford Blackwood's description but Carlton Blackwood's details, as she knew that her husband was travelling under his cousin's name. But it so happened that Carlton, too, was wanted in connection with a police enquiry at that time – so neither identity would have prevented Clifford being apprehended.

The marriage was doomed anyway. 'In the end', said Valerie, when commenting on their separation, 'he just wanted me to be a housewife, and I wasn't satisfied with that. Four years later we divorced.'

Four years after her wedding to Blackwood would have made the year 1986. But she said: 'When I got divorced in 1984 I was expecting Pierre, my second child. I was short of money, so I sold my four-bedroom house so that I could go on supporting Naomi.' Some time later she moved with her two children to a new house in Streatham's Becmead Road – and one of the first things she did was to have its exterior repainted in the same navy blue and white colour scheme as her former Drewstead Road home.

On 6 May 1993, I was approached by an informant with a tip-off about a man he suggested might prove interesting in connection with the quest to establish the identity of Naomi Campbell's long-lost natural father. A series of discreet enquiries culminated at the Old Bailey, where records about the man in question confirmed him to be Errol Lee Campbell, formerly Peter Errol Campbell, born 6 May 1951. The fact that the informant came to see me on Campbell's birthday was purely coincidental.

With a string of previous convictions to a name which he had changed by deed poll, including a three-year sentence in Frankfurt for drugs-related offences, Campbell was brought to trial at the Old Bailey aged thirty-nine charged with offences allegedly committed between 8 and 11 January 1988: namely, false imprisonment, rape, and buggery with a woman. The trial lasted six days. He was convicted on 20 August 1990 and sentenced the same day. Acquitted on the charge of false imprisonment, he was found guilty as charged of rape and buggery, and received an eight-year sentence on each account to be served concurrently. Representing him in his defence was Mr. D. J. Batcup for the solicitors Offenbach and Co. Campbell was remanded in custody, and lodged an appeal against the conviction on 25 September 1991.

He was lately being detained at the Norvic Clinic, a secure wing of St Andrew's Hospital, Thorpe, St Andrew's in Norwich, which is where I approached him, without success.

Checking records dating back to 26 July 1982, when Naomi's mother Valerie was in Geneva (a coincidence no doubt), we learn that Campbell had applied for a passport in order to travel to Switzerland, and was indeed granted a full British passport that year. He gave a Mitcham, Surrey home address, and his occupation as 'Menswear fashion designer'. Cross-checking the Surrey address, it was confirmed as the home of Eric and Pearline Campbell, Errol's parents, and their daughter Sandra.

A visit to this address brought us face to face with a short, plump West Indian lady who answered to the name Pearline, and who became hysterical when polite mention was made of the names Naomi, Valerie and Errol Campbell. She ordered us off her property, telling us we were mad and then threatened to 'pour acid' all over us, to 'burn our asses', and repeated over and over the words 'They'll sue me! You don't understand!' She told us she'd be deported and would lose everything. Not a single accusation or allegation had been made, but she refused to enter into conversation and threatened us again. We beat a hasty retreat. While we were waiting in the car and pondering how to proceed, Pearline again came out of her neat terraced house and approached the car. This time she tried to get her hands on us through the window and aggressively repeated over and over again the same phrases she'd already used.

We made some enquiries around the neighbourhood and spoke to a seventeen-year-old student whose identity we must protect here for obvious reasons, but who gave his address as being in the same street as the Campbells. He said he had lived at that address for ten years. When he learned that we were researching a biography of the supermodel Naomi Campbell, he exclaimed: 'Her grandparents live just up there!'

Throughout these extraordinary proceedings there had been one other player: a colourful 'intermediary' who, for one reason or another, is deeply involved and must remain nameless. At first he was anxious to cooperate but suddenly, without giving any explanation, he withdrew. It had become obvious to me throughout the months I had been dealing with him that this man had 'come to some arrangement' with Errol Campbell, and that the pair were clearly biding their time over something. Could it be that they believe there is money to be made here? Might they be holding out for a substantial offer from a newspaper for Errol's life story when he is released? The intermediary, who spoke with Errol Campbell in prison from a mobile phone, did not deny this. But why would another convicted rapist's life story be of such intense interest to the British press and indeed the general public?

'You don't understand', the intermediary said patiently. 'Mike Tyson is a rapist too . . .'

The foregoing does not establish that this man is Naomi's father and there are a couple of points to be made here. First, that the name Campbell in Jamaica is as common as Jones in Wales. Conclusions, therefore, cannot and must not be leapt to. Secondly, does the identity of Naomi Campbell's biological father really *matter*? Of course, it is something about her that people are fascinated by, if only to establish the other source of the genes that combined to give her such devastating beauty. But to all intents and purposes, Naomi has never had a real father.

3

P. Y. T.
(Pretty Young Thing!)

Even while Naomi was still tiny, Valerie could see something in her daughter that set her apart from the rest. A certain look, an attitude, a *je ne sais quoi*. Whatever it was it made Valerie's heart change gear whenever she thought about it. She was determined that Naomi would make the most of it, take every opportunity that came her way, have all the things that she herself had missed out on. A typical stage mother living unfulfilled ambitions through her child?

In the words of one leading American psycho-analyst whom I interviewed on the subject, 'To me the adult Naomi displays all the classic symptoms of a famous person who was pushed from a very early age by a parent – almost from the time she was born. This syndrome is best documented by Alice Miller in her book *Drama of the Gifted Child*. Such children tend to develop extremely narcissistic personalities later on. They have almost been forced into living out a parent's fantasies. There are many examples: Igor Stravinsky, Pablo Picasso, Michael Jackson, Brooke Shields. The parent's assessment of their child, even if it is subconscious, is: "You are here to fulfil *my* dreams." It can happen even while the child is still in the womb, and the parent may not even be fully aware of it. Nevertheless, this wish-fulfilment becomes the driving force in the relationship. Naomi's problem is compounded by the fact that only one of her real parents was at all involved in her upbringing – there was no one to balance the situation.'

It is one psycho-analyst's opinion, which others may contradict, but Valerie had indeed tried her best to raise herself, if not from the gutter then at least from the middle of the road. She'd had a stab at the good life, and who could blame her? She gave it her best shot, went as far as her looks and resources would carry her. But she had not made the big-time in the end – how many do? And anyway, things were different then. For Naomi, however, the time was right. She represented Valerie's chance at another crack of the whip. Her own dreams could well go full circle – and Valerie would continue to do everything in her power to make it come true.

'Jamaican women are always ambitious', explains Loanna Morrison of *The Voice*. 'It is in our blood. Because that blood is usually a mix of several different races – one family alone can be derived from Portuguese, Cuban, African, Spanish and English – we have that mixed ability, and a gut intelligence and wisdom which are rooted in a range of soils. It makes us much stronger, I think. We might not all be intellectuals, but we are certainly street-smart.

'What's more, black women, once they have children, become even more ambitious – for their kids. Also they tend to be much more cosmopolitan, more broad-minded, they already have that. And you know, you often find that famous black people were either orphans raised in children's homes, or brought up by a single mother. Their situation inspires them to do better for themselves. It gives them drive.'

Naomi, says Loanna, has everything to thank her mother for in terms of exploiting her assets to the hilt. 'If Valerie hadn't sent her to a school where they taught her deportment, and manners, and how to walk, she might never have made it. She was tall, but she could have looked very clumsy. Instead she learned how to walk tall and be graceful, and because of that her looks attracted a lot of attention. If Valerie hadn't gone off and danced her feet off all over Europe and paid for Naomi to have that education, she might not have become anything. She might have ended up on the supermarket check-out like all the others. You have to take your hat off to Valerie. Let's face it, it's pretty difficult being a single mother, even now. Things are better for us these days than they were for her. Back then, it was a hell of a lot harder for black women to get anywhere, do anything, buy property. When you think about what

Valerie achieved by herself, you can't help but admire her. I hope Naomi realizes that she owes her everything.'

As a toddler Naomi would watch, mesmerized, while her mother dolled up in tassels and sequins, plumes and pearls, and did a twirl before the bedroom mirror as she practised her routines.

'She was fascinated by the costumes and the way they moved,' remembered Valerie. 'By the time she was four, she was already saying that she wanted to be a dancer too. She just had to see a camera and she would start posing. And she loved dressing up. Even at four, she knew what she wanted to wear. If I put her in something she didn't feel right in, the tears would flow. Often she would dress herself and she'd come downstairs and you'd think, "Well, they go together", and you'd never have thought of putting them together yourself. Her colour schemes were perfect.'

It was a friend of Valerie's who suggested she should try to place her pint-sized coquette at a stage school. Val's sister June was able to recommend the Barbara Speake Stage School in East Acton, West London, which she had already selected for her own son, Naomi's cousin Paul. The school boasted among its former pupils rock singer Phil Collins, *Oliver* star Jack Wilde, kids' TV presenter Keith Chegwin and zany comic Brian Conley. Fees in those days were £100 per term from Form One, which had risen to £180 per term the year Naomi left. Phil Collins' mother June was actually the school's agent, based on the premises, which despite her grand age of seventy-something she remains to this day.

Miss Speake and Mrs Collins might be the Hinge and Bracket of stage schools: a glamorous, gutsy pair with a real show-must-go-on attitude to work and life. I spent a hilarious afternoon in their company, and they remembered their former pupil Naomi Campbell with fondness.

'Cute little kid, very, very quiet, didn't push herself, didn't bat an eyelid,' was Miss Speake's off-the-cuff recollection of Naomi, who had enrolled full-time at the school in January 1976, aged five, and left on 6 April 1984, when she was almost fourteen. Miss Speake had retained Naomi's school records, meticulously filed along with the others from her year in strict alphabetical order, and showed them to me to prove that she had remembered her dates correctly.

Miss Speake, a youthful sixty-four and the archetypal theatrical-looking stage school proprietress – owl-like gold-framed spectacles, dripping gilt earrings, diamond rings, appliquéd green tracksuit and glittering sandals – started her academy in a church hall forty-eight years ago when she was only sixteen. At first she offered classes exclusively in the performing arts – ballet was her forte, and she had been Royal Academy-trained – but for the past thirty-one years the school has also been a mainstream educational establishment and has changed location several times. June Collins, effervescent herself in multicoloured outfit and enormous coloured specs, had been associated with the school since her son Phil started there in 1961. Two years later, June joined forces with Barbara Speake when they launched the stage school proper with its own agency.

'I was a sixteen-year-old who thought she knew it all – and did,' Miss Speake told me. 'Mother said I didn't have any go about me – I'd learnt dancing but that was it. So I said "Right, I'll prove that I can do something and this is it."' Today the school has approximately 150 full-time students who wear a smart red uniform and study a full curriculum of academic subjects as well as drama, music and dance.

'Naomi came to the school because her mother wanted her to,' recalls Miss Speake emphatically. 'I remember the mother being very ambitious for the child. What a beautiful woman *she* was. She'd come in here sometimes looking stunning – incredible skin – and you'd look at yourself and think, "Oh Golly." They seemed to be living all over the place, they moved around a bit: Tulse Hill, Stockwell, then Streatham. The mother was a dancer, and Naomi was more or less brought up by her grandmother. The father I never heard of. They were not an interfering family – I hardly remember ever seeing them, and the mother was off touring most of the time. That dance troupe she was in was a bit sort of risqué. Very nice child, though. Quite an ordinary child really, when she got here – just ordinary. She was very slim. She sang quite well, I've got her on video – she sang her own little bit and she was quite delightful. But she was also quite laid back, she didn't shove herself in your face the way some children do – *me me me*!

'I never had any trouble with her, except that I was very disappointed when she left. She was just beginning to do her O-Level work, and that was totally interrupted. I believe she would definitely have got her O-Levels had she stayed on here. Naomi didn't actually want to leave – she was in tears on the last day here – but her mother wanted her to go to the Italia Conti because she thought she would do more dancing there. She definitely wanted her to be a dancer of some description – although she soon grew too tall to dance ballet professionally. I was more concerned with the education myself. I don't think she ended up doing very much education at Italia Conti at all! And she didn't like it there, I know for a fact, because she came back here a bit later. But I sent her packing. I said, "You've left, so leave." . . . The mother was probably anxious that she should follow in her footsteps.'

'At the time Naomi came here, we were working for Venture Studios in Covent Garden,' remembers June Collins. 'She did quite a bit of modelling, mostly mail-order catalogue work. She was always in the studio shooting those. We didn't have many "coloureds" them, and there wasn't so much work around for black children. But we got her quite a few acting, singing and dancing jobs. She did a few rock videos – *Quest for Fire*, with Bob Marley, and Pink Floyd's *The Wall*. And she was in *The Nightingale* with Sarah Brightman at the Lyric Theatre.'

Naomi also remembered being in the first British commercial for McDonald's, and even in the stage version of *The King and I* with Yul Brynner – but her teachers did not recall these assignments.

Julie Layton, Naomi's dancing teacher at Barbara Speake who taught her throughout the eight years she studied there, remembered Naomi as being 'very very pretty. She was just this lovely little thing. She was fairly shy, and very sweet, and she didn't say boo to a goose. She mixed well with the other children, though. She got on well, and she was quite popular, for a quiet one. She especially loved tap dancing. She was very good at that. But I wouldn't say dancing was her gift, her true field, not really. I remember one TV series we once did – poor Naomi was always being told off because she couldn't concentrate and dance at the same time, she was always a split second behind everyone else.

'We did a number of things with her, though. She danced in a six-week BBC comedy series, *Orville the Duck*. They actually came down to the school and chose the children themselves. She did *Brown Girl in the Ring*, and she was the one in the middle, in the ring. And not long before she left I remember her doing a Boy George video. . . . ' It was for the Culture Club single 'It's a Miracle', which was a Number 4 hit in 1984.

'Boy George actually came down here, and he still had all his hair then, and everyone went crazy for him,' remembers Julie. 'I believe that was the last thing she did here.'

The older she grew, the prettier she became. While most children seem to go through an ugly duckling phase in adolescence, Naomi slipped straight into swan-mode without so much as a waddle or a quack. She seemed to grow more beautiful by the week. By the time she was thirteen she was stunning, and her looks helped her to shed the shy streak which had perhaps held her back in childhood. Naturally graceful where others like her who suddenly shot up seemed gauche and gangly, she also began to develop a very strong and unique sense of style which helped her stand out from the crowd. She would walk into a room and jaws would drop. The others could only stand and stare.

'We did a school fundraiser in 1982-3,' remembers Miss Speake, 'and we asked for a whole load of second-hand clothes and did a fashion parade. The idea was to invite the parents and sell the clothes. I tell you, I have never seen anyone look so *gorgeous* as Naomi. She was in a baggy old pair of trousers, an old granddad shirt and a school tie, and she looked absolutely fantastic. What she did with those clothes was a miracle, really. No matter what you put her in, she could adapt it to her own personality and you'd sit and watch her and think, "Now why didn't I think of that?" Everything about the way she looked was perfect, from her height and her build to her posture, her hair, her face – everything. She used to have hair-pieces, little bits of jewellery – something, however small, to make herself different. She always stood out.

'Talent-wise, she didn't really have that much going for her. But she was always beautiful, always graceful, very well behaved, a very nice child indeed, who never showed off and who got on with her work. Not exactly a bundle of fun, but never a misery either. Yes, the press love to hate her now – but you *can't* actually hate her, there is nothing to hate. Of course she could have changed in the years since I last saw her, but I can't imagine she'd alter that much. People generally don't. It has a little to do with who you mix with later on, but not a lot. Naomi wasn't "full of herself" when she left here – she was simply self-confident and ready to make her way in life.'

Talking about her daughter's experiences at stage school, Valerie would later comment: 'Naomi has a lot to thank Miss Speake for. She didn't stand any nonsense. She always told them that if they wanted to do well they'd have to buckle under, and not waste their time if they thought showbusiness was a soft option. Naomi loved her. If she didn't get a job she would say she hadn't tried hard enough. She would say, "Mum, I haven't got to do my best but a hundred *times* my best." And I'd say, "And ten times *that*!" She wouldn't stop dancing, acting, singing. She used to tap dance in these incredibly loud American tap shoes in our garden and drive me absolutely crazy. At the end of term all her friends would come round and practise for the school show. It was a madhouse, but it was really fun.'

Even as an adolescent, Naomi seemed to have taken on board the painful truths of prejudice and had already faced up to the fact that she would have to strive all the harder to make it in what ethnic groups still considered to be a 'white man's world'. 'She'd say, "Mum, I know people say it's difficult for blacks, but it's what I want to do. Even if I've got to kick those doors down, I'll do it. I want to be an all-round entertainer and no one's going to stop me. I want to wear one of those big diamonds like Miss Speake's."' This was almost an echo of something Miss Speake herself had said years ago: that the door to success is labelled '*Push.*'

When she was twelve, Naomi begged her mother for extra dancing lessons on Saturdays at the high-profile Italia Conti Academy of Theatre Arts. Valerie agreed, and enrolled her daughter there as a part-time student. But not long afterwards, according to Valerie's account, Naomi evidently decided that it was time to spread her wings, and asked if she could leave Barbara Speake's and attend the Italia Conti full-time.

'Miss Speake had already told me she was going to make it. There was no way I could hold her back,' remembered Valerie. 'Before she took the entrance examinations, she asked me for a fiver and went down to the Pineapple dance studio to work out. For a week she drove me round the twist, singing and dancing. She was determined to get in, and she did.'

As legend would have it, Valerie then sold her precious four-bedroom Streatham home in order to afford the £750-a-term fees at the Italia Conti. Even Valerie herself would confirm this in several interviews, saying that she used the capital from the sale of the Drewstead Road house to buy a tip of a place, and that for a couple of months while it was being renovated the family moved to a one-bedroom rented flat. But when I queried this with Naomi during our interview, she snorted: 'Of course she didn't sell the house to pay my fees! She did sacrifice a lot for me, though, and she could have bought a big house with all the money she spent sending me to Italia Conti.'

In any event, the house was sold. Naomi would later add that she had wanted her mother to get rid of it because her Yorkshire terrier

Pepie had died there, and she didn't feel happy about being there
without him.

Naomi appears to have had a fairly liberal upbringing after her
mother returned from Europe and resumed caring for her daughter
as a full-time Mum. 'Mum was really easy-going,' Naomi recalled.
'She let us run round the house until the early hours, having midnight feasts and playing loud music. My mates could always sleep
over, and I was allowed to sleep at theirs, as long as she always knew
where I was. That's not to say that I didn't have discipline. I did.
Sometimes at night, even when I was so tired I just wanted to pass
out, she nagged and nagged me until I took my make-up off. Now,
no matter how tired I am, I always take all my make-up off. I have
never slept in it.'

Naomi was almost fourteen when she joined Conti's, first in
Stockwell and then in the Barbican, where her contemporaries included actress Emily Lloyd, later to make her name in the film *Wish
You Were Here*, and song-and-dance man Lionel Blair's model
daughter Lucy. Naomi's ambition was still to dance in her mother's
footsteps, or thereabouts. 'It would cross my mind now and again
that I might be a model, but I really wanted to be a jazz dancer.
When I eventually started modelling I didn't even know how to
pose, so I used ballet poses. Every summer, all summer long, I used
to tap dance in the garden and drive my Mum mad. But I loved
school. I thrived on being corrected and getting things right. I had
the most fun when I was dancing.'

Now a stunning young teenager who turned heads every time she
stepped outside her front door, Naomi was without doubt the pret-
tiest girl in her class. And she seemed to know instinctively that she
might be victimized because of that. So she launched herself on her
new classmates as the Naughty One, a bit of a jester, in order to off-
set the effects of her beauty on potentially jealous and bitchy classmates. It was a shrewd move, and it worked.

'I was very very shy, and although I knew a few people in the
school, I didn't know anyone in my class,' she said. 'So I started to

play pranks – you know, back-row-of-the-class stuff – and after a month or two I got to be liked. I loved that school so much,' Naomi said – contrary to Barbara Speake's impression of how her old pupil fared at her new school – 'although we drove the teachers up the wall. I used to look forward to going in so much that I would get up two hours early every morning. I even loved the uniform. It was very important to me to get on and be successful. I used to say to my Mum, "Don't worry, I promise I won't let you down." And I used to tell all my friends at Italia Conti, "I just have to do good for my Mum."

'Conti's played a big part in how my life turned out. When you're a teenager you learn things. I think I became more feminine when I was there, more of a woman. I was just finding out about myself and what I wanted to do and pursue. The school taught me how to deal with people and how to handle situations. It taught me posture, how to present myself, and to be polite.'

As hard as she studied at Italia Conti, Naomi made plenty of time for fun with her friends. Apart from the usual giggly-schoolgirl sky-larking, such as putting drawing pins on teachers' chairs and pro-voking the more volatile members of staff – one Chinese teacher there was said to be in the habit of hurling the blackboard across the classroom when she could take no more – once a week the 'hard core' of the 'Class of '86' would make their way down to Tiffany's nightclub in Wimbledon, where they danced, drank Coca Cola, ran away giggling if they were chatted up by boys, and sat gossiping on the shelf in the ladies' toilets. In much the same way as most young teenagers spend their free time, Naomi and her friends would hang out at McDonald's, and at each other's houses. At Naomi's, they probably got away with more than their own mothers would ever stand for at home.

She would hang around most of the time with her best friends from school, Samantha Lewis and Suzanne Howard. She and Samantha lived near one another, and travelled to and from school together. They would take the 159 bus to Brixton station and then travel by

Tube to the Barbican. By the time they reached the Underground they had often met up with other classmates, and fellow travellers were not unfamiliar with the sight of a gaggle of ten or more Italia Conti pupils on the train together, giggling and screaming.

'But Naomi would kind of keep control,' remembered Samantha. 'Whenever we started getting too riotous, she would play Mum, stand up and tell us all to quieten down. Heaven help anyone who pushed her on the Tube – the look she gave them! She would really scowl. She just hated being pushed around. And whenever she got annoyed her incredibly long arms would start flying around.'

Samantha kept a scrapbook of photographs and newspaper cuttings about her famous friend. She has the shots from Naomi's first 'grown-up' professional modelling job, for *Looks* magazine, depicting her friend in a variety of young-fun outfits. Samantha, who won a scholarship to the school, became deputy head girl and starred in TV's children's series *Grange Hill* for more than five years. She would later recall Naomi's excitement when they spotted the magazine on sale at a news-stand outside Brixton station as they were coming home from school. Naomi started shrieking and jumping up and down on the pavement, yelling, 'Look, Sam! It's me, it's me!'

'I'm so glad she was in our year,' said Samantha later, 'because she was mad, totally mad. She was really genuine and nice.' The pair spent plenty of time together outside school hours, dreaming about the future and confiding in each other their secret hopes and fears. 'Naomi always wanted to follow in her mother's footsteps – she always wanted to be a dancer or a model. But she never really dressed up unless we were going out. She's beautiful and tall, but you wouldn't think so by the clothes she used to wear. She was a little bit obsessed with her looks, especially her hair. And heaven help her if she ever got a spot. Once she got one on her forehead, and she put so much TCP on that she burned it.'

Other pupils remembered Naomi as a dominant character. One told me: 'She always had to have her say. And if she had something to say, there was no shutting her up – she'd go right ahead and come out with it whatever the consequences. You couldn't ignore her. If she was in the room, you were always aware of it. She was just one of those people who always stand out in a crowd. She was always great to look at, and she made the best of herself, so you can imagine how amazing she was, really. I would have died to have legs like Naomi, but you could do without her arms. In dance classes you kept out of her way – her bloody arms were all over the place.

'I think we all knew she would end up being someone. She just had this thing about her, like she always knew it was going to happen and it was only a matter of time. I think she always took it for granted that she would be really famous, and I suppose that's why she is.'

Suzanne Howard remembered Naomi as a rebellious type, too. But she claimed Naomi's naughty behaviour was nothing compared to that of their classmate Emily Lloyd's. 'Emily was crazy at school, she really was. She would come to school with her tights ripped, and at ballet she never had her ballet shoes or her hair in a bun. We all used to dream of making films and meeting Matt Dillon, and now, for her, it's like a dream come true.'

As if to pay homage to the St Trinian's tradition, the girls were all adept at restyling their school uniforms to reflect the latest fashions. Skirts would be taken in and up, high heels would be worn, and they sported more make-up in school than out, especially lipstick – the weirder and more wonderful the better. Naomi, of course, was always different. As one girl remembered, Naomi always had *Vogue* in her bag when the others were still reading *Just Seventeen*. And she would never be seen dead in a pair of court shoes.

'I wore Doctor Marten boots to school, which I got in Shelley's on the King's Road, and I went to the Sock Shop in Covent Garden for frilly little socks to wear with them!' Naomi told me. 'I suppose I did always have that edge when it came to a look. My mother helped me a lot there. She actually bought all my clothes until I was at least fourteen years old, and I really loved all the stuff she got me. Some girls *hated* their mothers buying them clothes – they had no idea. But not me. My mother always had a lot of style, and still does.'

On one occasion, when pupils were asked to choose a topic and give a mini-lecture to the rest of the class, Naomi gave clues as to what she would soon be doing for a living. Her subject was modelling. She shared make-up tips, gave an exaggerated demonstration of how to slink along a catwalk and how to enter a room – hip-bones first – and had the whole class in stitches.

'She was a natural comedienne', remembered another girl from her year. 'She had this way of dropping into a slightly different tone of voice when she felt a bit self-conscious about what she was saying. She didn't always know what she was doing, but it was very, very funny. Naomi was always the type of girl people hung around – she would always make you laugh.'

Charlotte Plent, who acted in *Annie*, appeared in several TV series and went on to become head girl of Italia Conti, also remembered Naomi as one of the funniest girls in the school. 'She was mad – but in a nice way,' she would later recall. 'I think she was hyperactive. She would come bouncing into the room. She was always jumping about, really excited. We *were* a bit of a naughty class. Everyone had their own personality, and some were very, very funny. We were always getting told off for laughing.

'When Naomi first came to the school you could tell she would go into modelling. She was just perfect for it – her figure, her height, everything. She stuck up for me once when I got into trouble for something I hadn't done. That was typical of her nature. You could have an argument with her one day and the next day she would stick up for you.'

In those days, the girl who would go on to capture the hearts of some of the world's most eligible males had little time for boys. Apart from the fact that most of the lads in her class were a year younger than her anyway, at that age she simply wasn't interested in the charms of the opposite sex.

'She never went out during the week,' recalled Valerie, 'and when she did, it was always to do with her ambition. She would go to the Italia Conti school at 7.30 a.m., and then after school I'd take her to extra lessons in Kingston, and at the Pineapple Studio. It was go, go, go. She didn't stop. I'd pick her up later and she'd be home at about 9.30 p.m. She never complained about the distances she had to travel, and she was never late for school. She worked hard. Boys couldn't have been further from her mind.'

She would, of course, eventually make up for lost time – and how. She always had a thing about pop stars, even then, but in those days she worshipped them from the middle distance. 'I loved, loved, *loved* Boy George,' Naomi told me. 'I was a *huge* fan when I was about fourteen. And I adored Jon Moss,' she said of Culture Club's dark-eyed drummer.

'It was always Jon Moss with Naomi,' remembered Samantha Lewis. 'She had pictures of him plastered all over her bedroom wall – she even engraved his name on her wardrobe.'

'I was a real groupie in those days,' said Naomi. 'I used to go up to their homes – Alma Place, Abercorn Close, after school and sit outside for hours. Jon had the mews, and George had a flat in one of the houses. I collected pictures of George from magazines – any tiny picture I saw in *Smash Hits*, anything to do with Boy George – and I waited outside his house until he'd come out and sign them. Then I'd go home. I had a whole box of stuff, and he'd signed the lot.'

Who knows what became of Jon Moss following the demise of Culture Club? But George O'Dowd is a survivor and has held his own, scoring a recent hit with the theme song from the acclaimed feature film *The Crying Game*.

'I'm still a huge fan,' Naomi admitted. 'I still think he's got the best voice – and he sounds better than ever. I did two of his videos – *I'll Tumble 4 Ya*, and *It's a Miracle*. Some time later we were doing a show for Katherine Hamnett and I finally had the nerve to tell him that I was his biggest fan, and that it was me who used to sit on his doorstep all the time. He just laughed, he thought it was sweet. I'd love him to write a song for me, do a duet with him or something. I think I'm gonna ask!'

Modelling for Anna Sui's Biba-inspired collection

Above: Round two with Mike Tyson

Trapped in the elevator with Steven Meisel

Dancing with Madonna at
Naomi's 21st birthday party

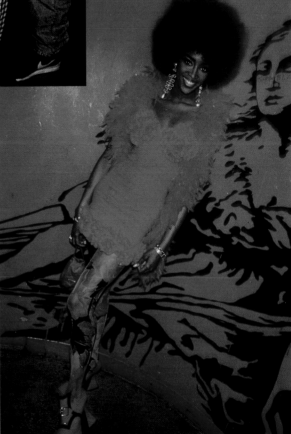

At the birthday party for record
producer Jellybean Benitez

Queen of the Catwalk in Lagerfeld for Chanel, Spring 1993

4

Something in the Way
She Moves

Hype is someone else's paid enthusiasm for something about which you might, at best, be ambivalent. It is what publicists do for a living, and journalists occasionally fall for. It is about turning an unknown into the Next Big Thing – and the thing we all assumed must be behind Naomi's rise and rise to fame.

We were wrong. If you have read a dozen times that she was discovered in Covent Garden one day while out buying tap dancing shoes with her best friend Suzanne, you were not having the hype pulled over your eyes yet again. It is a story that smacks of Cinderella and sounds awfully far-fetched, but that is because it is true.

'I *was* discovered in Covent Garden hanging out after school!' says Naomi. 'A lady called Beth Boldt who used to run an agency called Synchro, and who's American, came running up and gave me her card. I actually thought she was going to one of my other friends, Suzanne, who had long blonde hair and blue eyes, but she came right up to *me* and said, "Come and see me, I'm just up there."' Little did poor Suzanne Howard know then that she was destined to become the 'Pete Best' of the modelling world, while her friend would wind up as famous as the Beatles.

It takes an angel's face and the figure of a goddess to turn the head of a jaded model agent who has seen the lot in her time. But something made Beth Boldt look twice. What she saw was a gangly, tangly schoolgirl in uniform, slender as a willow wand, with toffee-coloured gossamer skin and a knock-out smile. An elongated slip of a giggly thing nudge-nudging with her girlfriends. Young, un-self-conscious, *irresistible*, she would go so far as to say – though Beth could not explain why. They never can, model agents, they just know when they see one. It's a kind of magic with a special smell that only agents seem to have the nose for. Naomi Campbell was the best she had happened upon in an age.

'I couldn't take my eyes off her,' remembered Beth, who in 1985 still owned her own London model agency, Synchro, eventually to be bought out by Elite. But she wasn't even out on the prowl that afternoon – she was just minding her own business. Suddenly, she found herself feasting her eyes on a vision. 'She had these *long* legs – and her skin just radiated. She had an incredibly good clothes figure – even in her school uniform. You could see the broad shoulders and little hips. She was majestically beautiful.'

Naomi was as stunned by the encounter as Beth. 'She just dashed up to me in the street, like in a film or something, and introduced herself. She said she was a model agent and thought I could be a model. I didn't think I looked very attractive – how *can* you in your school uniform? But she gave me her card, asked me to come in or give her a ring if I was interested, and walked off. I just took the card home and gave it to my Mum.'

Thus began the big dilemma for Valerie as she weighed up the pros and cons. Naomi was still only fifteen. Surely they had more time? Together they had worked so hard to achieve a break like this, but now that it was here, she was not sure if she could bring herself to deal with it. Not *yet*. Exasperated by her mother's reluctance to make a decision, Naomi finally confronted her and they sat down and considered all the options together.

'I actually told her to leave it for a while and finish school,' admitted Valerie. 'But then a few months later, Beth phoned me. Naomi had apparently sneaked into her agency one day after school and said, '*You* phone my Mum!'

Valerie was worried that her daughter's feet would leave the ground, and that her innocence would be snatched away overnight. 'I didn't like the idea of all those trips abroad one bit,' she admitted. 'I didn't know if she could handle it, whether people would take advantage of her, and I wasn't at all keen on the idea of her leaving school. But in the end I trusted Beth 100 per cent. I had to.'

According to Beth Boldt, encouraging a young girl to cut short her education for the sake of a modelling career which might not work out is not a decision she has ever taken lightly. 'It wasn't easy for me to tell Naomi that she ought to quit school and go in for modelling, because modelling can sometimes last only six months,' she said. 'But it wasn't as though she had always wanted to be a lawyer or a doctor. She had always wanted to be in the entertainment business, and that had a lot of bearing on our decision. Naomi was definitely unique. Not only did she have the looks, but a great talent that one sees only in exceptional girls: she could *move*. She could really show clothes and she had charisma and excitement. So many girls are physically beautiful, but personality-wise they are as dull as ditchwater.' Unable to reach a compromise, they decided to pursue both careers for a while and see what happened.

A perfectionist even in those days, Naomi found her height still got the better of her sometimes, and she had fretted for some time over the way she walked. Finally, she went to her mother and said she needed special tuition. 'She suddenly said she had to learn how to walk gracefully, and would I send her to deportment classes,' recalled Valerie. 'I told her I couldn't afford it, so she said, "Right, I'll go and get a job and I'll pay for it myself." That was when she went to Top Shop in the West End. She borrowed my leather and suede suit for the interview, and she ruined it. It was covered in make-up stains.'

Togged up in her mother's best, with seamed stockings and stiletto heels, Naomi was fifteen going on twenty-one when she tottered into Top Shop and applied for a Saturday job. 'I really needed the money, so I lied about my age and said I was seventeen,' she says. 'They took one look at me and gave me a job on the spot.'

The wages were £1.92 per hour. For that, Naomi had to keep the clothes racks in order and spend endless hours manning the till. It was mind-numbingly dull work but she did it with a smile, and stashed away her earnings until she had saved enough to pay for her lessons. Then she enrolled at the Judi James Modelling School in Chelsea and acquired the final skill which would equip her for catwalk stardom.

'Catwalk courses' are short, sharp and to the point. Most model 'wannabes' learn everything they need to know in one week. A model agency will often send new girls on such a course at their own expense, perhaps recouping the fees from their earnings later on.

At Judi James, Naomi learned a good deal more than how to walk across a room with a book balanced on her head. She learned that good deportment tells the world how you feel about yourself. That pride in one's appearance indicates supreme self-confidence, perhaps the most seductive quality in a woman. Models, her tutor would explain, are clothes hangers. And if you put a fabulous outfit on a bent-up hanger, it is not going to look any good. First, Naomi learned, comes good posture: SHH! – that is, Shoulders over Hips over Heels. She was tall, but she had to think even taller – be tall mentally as well as physically.

She learned that it is vital to move gently and slowly – to glide, almost – always keeping the line of the clothes in mind. That clothes have their own personality, and that a good model *becomes* the clothes she wears, adapting her own character to complement the garment. The chameleon in Naomi picked up on this immediately, and she articulated it later on in her career.

'Everything I put on feels different,' she said. 'It's like a different character. It is very important to recognize this. There's no way I would walk the same in every outfit I've worn on the runway all these years. Azzedine is totally different from St Laurent, is different from Ozbek. That's why they book the same few models over and over again for the shows, because we are the ones who can differentiate between each designer that we work for. When you're in Chanel you look like a Chanel model. When it's Alaia you look like an Alaia model. Believe me, it is harder than it looks.'

As another young model put it, more bluntly: 'If you're walking along in a bloody tight dress and high heels, it is gonna change the way you are! It's different again when they put you in something more funky. I try not to let the clothes take me over, though. You still have to be yourself – I reckon it's you wearing the clothes, not the clothes wearing you. I find that the music, more than the clothes, gives me the atmosphere, and I change my mood to fit that.'

First, of course, Naomi had to learn the tricks of the trade. Her tutors back at the Judi James Modelling School clearly made a good job of teaching her. She learned how to shed garments gracefully while actually strutting up and down the catwalk; and that remaining cool, calm and sophisticated as you extricate yourself from a designer jacket is no mean feat. Try it: you have to get it off the shoulders, take the hands out of the sleeves, then with one graceful movement of the wrist the jacket comes up in the air and you catch it in the middle – just like that! Who said it was easy?

Then there's the intricate half-turn. The models made it look like falling off a log, but they practise until they are blue in the feet. Pivot on the balls, keep pivoting, don't pick up that left foot! Spin, go on, until your legs are crossed and it feels really uncomfortable, and *then* you're home and dry. . . .

Catwalk modelling is worth a cool mint to a Supermodel who masters the art *and* can manage it in a stuffy room to blaring music, with hundreds of pairs of eyes all focused on her, and not lose her nerve. Holding a long pose, putting up with being poked and prodded and taped and pinned into all kinds of shapes you were never designed for, and maintaining the illusion that you are having a great time, is not as easy as it looks. But that, of course, is why they pay them so much money.

One of the first procedures a new model will be subjected to is the 'test shot' session, from which her Comp Card will be produced. This is an A5-size business card, also known as a 'Z-card', featuring her best shots – usually a head shot plus some 'action' or editorial pictures. Comp cards are then sent out to photographers, magazines and other clients and are effectively used to gain a model more work.

Beth Boldt recalled the first test pictures that were taken of Naomi. She was, said Beth, halfway through her hair and make-up session when in walked the photographer, Koto Boloso, and he did a double-take. 'His first words were: "*Look* at her, she is so beautiful and strong. We must photograph her *raw!*' Off came all the make-up and the hairpiece, and Naomi was incredible. She looked so earthy.'

A new model will do quite a few 'test' photo sessions in the early days to get pictures for her portfolio, or 'book'. In a test session, the model works for nothing in return for pictures, or sometimes she will be asked to pay for just the film and prints. The photographer, fashion stylist, hair and make-up artists also work for nothing in return for the model's pictures to help build up their own portfolios. One of Naomi's very first such sessions was booked by photographer Gary Compton amd make-up artist Denise Lilley, who worked together regularly on a variety of teenage magazines – *Jackie*, *My Guy*, *Patches* and *Just Seventeen*. The session was to be shot in a St John Street, Farringdon studio one afternoon after school. They had booked her from a photocopy obtained from Beth Boldt's Synchro agency: her Comp Card was not yet even available, as she had only been with the agency for one week.

'Gary and I had a theme, a scene that we had agreed on for the test shoot we wanted to do, and were flipping through all the new Xeroxes that had come in – Xeroxes featuring new models are sent in practically every week,' Denise told me. 'For a test you'd generally pick a model with a lot of potential, because you're going for something different that will ultimately get you more work. Naomi's Xerox, which featured a full-length shot and a head shot, just stood out from the rest. She was exceptional. . . . This was the mid-eighties, and I have to say there were not that many black models to choose from at that time. It's a fact that most of the agencies were pushing white girls. We particularly wanted a dark-skinned girl for the shot we had in mind, and we looked at a few. Naomi definitely had something the others didn't.'

Whatever it was, Denise could not put a name to it. But both she and the photographer recognized that day that Naomi was special. 'Well, at that time she had a very innocent yet knowing look about her,' says Denise. 'Whoever signed her up knew they had something there. It might sound odd, but you should also be able to tell from the Xerox what kind of thing you might be able to do with a particular model, and we both just knew she had it.

'On the day she turned up after school. She was still wearing her uniform and I was a bit taken aback – it was the first time I had ever been on a shoot when the model has turned up in school uniform. And she was *so* nervous! It was quite late in the afternoon, there were just the three of us in the studio, and we were well aware of the fact that we were dealing with a fifteen-year-old girl. I actually felt slightly sorry for her, and I know Gary did as well.

'My first reaction when I saw her was, "Oh God, she's a lot taller than I thought." But she held herself really well, and I said to her, "Do you dance?" She broke out in smiles and said, "Yes! I'm a ballet dancer and I've done tap, that's what I really love." She seemed very pleased that I spotted this about her. What actually made me notice it was that she had really bony feet!

'She started chatting to me about school while I was doing her make-up – I didn't do much with her hair – and said, "I love my school but it's ever so difficult to try and go here, go there, do this modelling when I'm still studying." But at the same time she was really excited about it all – she *wanted* to be doing it. She told me that her Mum was in showbusiness, that she had always wanted to be a dancer just like her, and that it was her Mum who had made her go in that direction and really encouraged her to get on.'

The session involved a cave scene with a very earthy look for the model. 'Naomi wasn't 100 per cent happy with the pictures that we were going to do,' admits Denise. 'She was quite firm about not doing anything too raunchy or seductive – not that we really wanted that – but her attitude impressed us, coming from such a young girl. She was obviously in control even then. We wanted to take her back to the beginning, give the shot a "cave girl" look without being that obvious. She needed to look as natural as possible, but to give it an eighties' feel too. Not easy, but she went along with it, and whatever we asked her to do she was happy to cooperate. Again for such a young girl, she was really professional. She was almost too helpful, in fact. The scene we put her in was quite a lot to expect even from an experienced full-time model, never mind a part-timer who had only just started. We were really pleased with the session, but the pictures were never actually published.' Denise retains the transparencies to this day.

Soon afterwards came the 'big break' that all models dream of. And, like all the best opportunities, it was such a time-honoured cliché that it might have been lifted straight from a rags-to-riches blockbuster by Jackie Collins. Just three months after signing with Beth Boldt's Synchro model agency, Naomi found herself on a States-bound jet, booked on her first assignment for British *Elle* magazine. The job was actually hers by default, because another model had cancelled at the last moment. Naomi, an unwitting understudy, stepped straight from the wings into her shoes. Who cared? Naomi couldn't have made a better first impression. After that, there would be no turning back.

As her mother Valerie remembered, 'I desperately wanted to go with her, but I was pregnant with my little boy Pierre, so I just couldn't manage it. But there was no holding Naomi back, she was raring to go.'

It was Lucinda Chambers, then senior fashion editor of *Elle*, who had hired her for the job on the spot. 'I was going to Alabama the next day and the model I'd booked had just cancelled,' said Chambers in a 1991 interview. 'Naomi rolled in and I couldn't believe how beautiful and graceful this girl was. There was something about the way she moved that I knew would work well on the page – and she had a great body, very lean and toned.'

When the fashion editor went round to Naomi's Streatham home to pick her up on the way to the airport, she found her mother handing out pocket money for the trip. 'She was fifteen, and I don't think she'd ever been abroad before.'

Everyone involved in the shoot was bowled over by this smiley new girl, and couldn't wait to congratulate her agent on such a 'find'. Beth Boldt was bowled over by their reaction. 'The editor rang me and said, "Beth, this girl is a star!" The photographer rang and said he'd never worked with anyone so sweet and nice. The booker phoned and said, "This girl is just amazing! What a personality! She never stops beaming!" Compared with other models who can be really difficult, Naomi was a breath of fresh air.'

The glitz and glamour of the trip might have got the better of her – this was probably the most exciting thing she had ever done in her life, after all – and who could have blamed her for that? It didn't, though. Naomi still found time to sit down and dash off a few postcards to her friends and family in London. To Samantha Lewis, who still treasures the card, she wrote in unpunctuated schoolgirl scrawl: "Hi Sam, I am having a wonderful time working for Elle magazine I have been to five [sic] states in America Florida Mississippi Alabama New York New Orleans gulf of Mexico tell Miss Healey and everyone Hello see you soon the weather here is in its 80s Love and Cuddles Naomi xxx'

The card was postmarked 24 April 1986. The now fully fledged model was not even Sweet Sixteen. But within a year she would be living in Manhattan, and setting her sights on the catwalks and magazine covers of the world.

5

I'll Take Manhattan

Never was a model agent's job made easier. Some nit-picking bookers moaned about the tiny scar on her face to the side of Naomi's nose, and she was under considerable pressure to have it surgically fixed. But such imperfections become a model's trademark – such as Cindy Crawford's famous mole. Others criticised Naomi's lips for being too big – one magazine executive even cruelly referred to her as 'Baboon-Bum Gob', because the way she often painted her mouth resembled nothing so much as an ape's anus!

But on the whole the industry's response to Beth Boldt's new girl Naomi was overwhelming, and very soon her modelling assignments were running back-to-back.

During that heady first year she also worked a great deal in Paris, where she became a kind of live-in muse model – the perfect, inspirational body to fit the clothes – for designer Azzedine Alaia, the man who has since often been described as Naomi's 'father-figure'. Alaia became stuck with the tag because he has always referred to his favourite models as his 'daughters' – about ten internationally known girls to whom he gives a lot of highly covetable free clothes, and some of whom he even allows to use his home as their Paris base. One such favourite is Naomi, whom he tucked under his wing almost from the moment she first arrived in France to model for him.

'Azzedine has been great to me,' Naomi told me. 'He's very kind to all his girls. When I first went to Paris I didn't speak any French, and he really looked after me. When I had all my money stolen he said he thought I'd better come and stay at his house, and I did. He made that first year so much easier for me by making me feel secure.'

As much as the capital of chic captured her innocent imagination, Naomi already had her sights set on the brighter lights of a much bigger city. It was inevitable. Every model worth her blemish concealer knew that if you were going to make it major league, you had to get yourself to New York. If she doesn't even give it a try, she can't want it that much, so goes the saying. It was only a matter of months before Naomi, now working regularly for Alaia and Yves St Laurent as well as doing more than her fair share of editorial work, started toying with the idea of the Big Move. Even at sixteen, her drive and ambition were palpable. Bethann Hardison, who met Naomi shortly after she signed with Beth Boldt, remembered: 'We'd go out to dinner, and Naomi would say, "Bethann, if I come to New York, could you help me get on *The Cosby Show?*" ' Hardison did, helping Naomi land a bit-part on an episode in 1988.

Fashion editors are the first to admit that there is more work for a model in New York than perhaps anywhere else in the world. As Lowri Turner of the London *Evening Standard* explains, 'All the big stores have major advertising campaigns, and a lot of the companies are actually based there – cosmetics houses, mail order companies – so that is where they hold the castings. Also, the strongest model agencies in the world are based there – Fords, Elite. On top of that, a lot of fashion shoots are done in Miami and the Caribbean, which are much more accessible from New York than Europe. It really is at the heart of the fashion and beauty worlds.'

But at what stage in her career, if at all, should a model take the transatlantic plunge? Lowrie admits that most girls are usually far too young to go when they do, but that the move is more or less compulsory if she is to succeed. 'Usually a girl will do six months to a year in Europe before trying for New York.' Even the Supermodels' Supermodel, Linda Evangelista, did her time and paid her dues in Paris.

'You go to Paris to "get pictures for my book",' says Lowri. 'What they mean by that is to do things that are interesting and artistic, because they need to have an aura of the Mood of the Moment about the portfolio that represents them, and you don't really get that anywhere else. If a girl starts out in London, she will establish "the face", to a certain extent. Then move on to Paris, Hong Kong or New York to earn the big money. Not so many London models actually uproot and move permanently to another country, though. Most of them don't live in one place anyway, because they are constantly on the move. It's a mad Romany lifestyle for a few years for most of them, and then out.'

What kind of a mother allows her sixteen-going-on-seventeen-year-old daughter to leave home and start a new life in another country, let alone one of the world's more hazardous domains? In Valerie's case, one who can hardly say no – because she had done exactly the same thing herself. Besides, Valerie was probably as aware as Naomi that top models do not hang out on Streatham High Road. They reinvent themselves in New York, Milan or Paris and lead charmed, perfumed lives on the arms of the world's most desirable males. If Naomi was going to stand a chance at making it as a grade one model, she *had* to go – and fast. The fashion industry does not hang around waiting for a new girl to be mature enough to leave home. It finds another one.

That Naomi was so eager to go says much about her maturity and drive as a teenager, as well as about the way she was perceived by those around her. Had her mother not believed she could cope away from home, Valerie would never have let her go – or at least she might have attempted to uproot herself and her small son and go with her, the more likely option for a typical 'stage mother'. For Naomi, it was the most exciting move in an already fairly eventful life.

'I am in love with New York, I have never stopped loving it,' she told me when we met there. 'This city fulfils your wildest dreams. Obviously I travel all the time. From here I go everywhere to do my job. But this is my base.'

But it's so far away from home . . . from her mother, her grandmother, her little brother. She doesn't have any real family here

. . . didn't she sometimes get just a little homesick?

'*No!*' She means it. But sheer geography means that, more often than not, she is forced to rely on friends whenever she gets lonely. 'Yes – you do to an extent,' she admits. 'But actually I don't rely on anyone. I'm not dependent on other people to make me happy. I've always been told that I must learn to make myself happy. I believe in that.'

Her drive and confidence are assets she truly believes she was born with. 'I don't think I'd be here otherwise. But I've never been afraid of trying something new. My mother was apprehensive, of couse, but she would never have tried to stop me. She has always wanted for me what I want for myself. She was travelling all over Europe to get her career going when she was sixteen. She understood. It was in the blood. It might seem strange to other people that she let me come. But when I first arrived I did live with my agent, so I was perfectly safe. Shortly afterwards I switched agencies and signed with Elite, because I had known the owner, John Casablancas, since Paris and really liked him. So I went to him. I'm still with Elite and I still like him a lot!

'I can't say my Mum wasn't worried, because she was. But I kept in constant contact, and still do. We speak all the time. My mother knows what I'm like, and that I won't end up on the wrong side of the tracks.'

Significantly, though, if she could change one thing about her current lifestyle, it would be ' . . . to have my family closer to me. Would I move them out here? They'd like to. My Mum comes out often, she really likes New York. She agrees with me that it doesn't really compare with anywhere else. California? No way! I don't like the West Coast very much. I like going out there to work, but I couldn't live there. Here is more happening. Out there it's all "What's your name, what do you do, what's your sign, what gym do you go to?" No – I'm joking.' She's not!

'Is this my ideal place in the whole world to live? It is for now, yes. I'm based here as a model, this is home.'

There is no indigenous population in New York – not really. Everybody here is from somewhere else. Nobody belongs, but everyone fits in, by virtue of the fact that they made the effort to get here in the first place. Here is the perfect place to start reinventing yourself, and that is precisely what Naomi set out to do whilst never denying her past. She could hardly have achieved this without leaving home. If you can make it here, you'll make it anywhere, says Frank Sinatra. It is a long way from Streatham to the gut of Manhattan – but not far enough, if you ask her.

The New York that Naomi first landed in was a very different city from the more hard-up, Recession-battered version she lives in today. In the 1980s, when she took Manhattan, it was like hitting the jackpot. There was never a better time to arrive – and everything was open. In the right circles, money was no object. Ronald Reagan was in the White House, people were making big dough and they were spending it, too. Those were the days of extremely lavish lifestyles, the heyday of high society, media and entertainment, and parties that lasted for three days, plane tickets thrown in. Enormous wealth was not even confined to showbusiness: everyone was at it. Wall Street, the junk bonders, the leverage buy-out guys – you name them, they were having a good time.

Such was the backdrop against which a few top models took their first sassy steps towards world stardom. International media coverage of the fashion Collections had recently given rise to the term 'Supermodel', which was represented by a high-profile group including Linda Evangelista and Cindy Crawford. These girls were barely twenty-something, but there was absolutely no mistaking them: they were literally dripping in power price tag outfits from de la Renta and Chanel – *and* letting the world know how seriously rich they were.

'They carried themselves like queens,' said Elsa Klénch, host of CNN's fashion news programme *Style*. 'They brought a kind of glamour to the city and indeed to the fashion business that had been missing for years.' In perfect step with the late eighties, the go-get-it

Supermodels were the personification of the New York lifestyle at that time. And it was into this very glittering fold that the teenage Naomi Campbell was welcomed with open arms. She slotted right in without a backward glance. Naomi had made it, and she had it made.

She was from London, so she was special from the outset: everyone was interested in her if only for that reason. She was coddled by her big-sister buddies Linda Evangelista and Christy Turlington, cossetted by her model agency and clucked over by Bethann Hardison, who had by now become such a dear friend that she accompanied Naomi to church on an irregular basis – they attended the famous Abyssinian Baptist church in Harlem, whose Pastor is the Rev. Calvin Butts, feted throughout New York as a flamboyant black 'Pope'. He conducted the Eddie Murphy nuptials at the Plaza Hotel, and is part of the Black New York Society of which Naomi was instantly an honorary member.

Naomi was not particularly religious, and had not been much of a churchgoer in England, even though her mother made quite a thing of her own faith. But in America, a token belief has certain social advantages which simply cannot be ignored. The Campbell and Hardison families periodically took vacations together, and Valerie's mind was at ease knowing that her daughter had, at least, a reliable chaperone in the city to whom she could run for cover if she found she could no longer cope.

New York, of course, has never been representative of the rest of America. It is actually an island off its shores. You must pass through a tunnel or over a bridge to get to Manhattan, hence the term 'Bridge and Tunnel' to denote out-of-towners and separate them from the In-Crowd. These are New York's only links to the rest of a very different country. Forty per cent of Manhattan's residents, according to recent statistics, were born in a country other than America. Some seventy different languages are spoken in the city.

It is a mixture which makes Brixton's seem bland. But what would have been a teenage Londoner's first perceptions of the differences between home and New York?

'At the beginning I was totally dazzled by everything,' Naomi told me. 'The size, the extremes, the choices in everything. I was very excited to be here. But at times the fact that I was actually living in the most exciting city in the world was mind-boggling.' Sensory overload? Not the word for it! 'For example, I couldn't believe the TV channels. There were more than sixty. Yes, most of it was crap, and there were adverts all the time, cut right into the programmes. It all merges into one thing coming at you, and in the end you don't know if you are watching the programme or the advert.'

Cory, a retired English model from Islington in North London who at eighteen made the same move as Naomi, still lives in New York City, though now married with children. She often found herself drinking in the same bars and dancing in the same clubs as the teenage Naomi – smart venues that would open and close down within the month. 'She was a lot like me – she really went for it,' Cory remembers. 'When you first get here, you stay out all night and go from place to place. Everyone did. I would even take the subway home at 3 a.m., which I would never do now, but when you first arrive you are terribly naive and totally fearless.'

The brazenness of the city could be mind-boggling to a teenager so far away from home. Sex shows on TV advertising the services of prostitutes. Naked chat shows. Drugs sold openly on the streets: marijuana, crack, cocaine, heroin – you name it, it was there to be bought. It was, says English celebrity photographer Nick Elgar, who made the move to New York ten years ago, a place that made a naive Londoner grow up overnight.

'I remember feeling that the last shreds of my youthful innocence just vanished when I got here,' he says. 'Basically, anything you wanted to try was available. There was so much temptation. But there were also people begging on the streets and on the subway at a level I never remember seeing in London. The hookers bang on car windows at traffic lights and show you their tits. And then you realize half of them are *guys*. . . . I was so naive, I didn't know from trans-sexuals or transvestites, but I soon did. I learned what's what. In New York you have to. It's a dangerous city and it's too easy to be immune to that side of it. Everybody you know has been mugged. Most have survived a threatening incident. I never knew what gunfire sounded like until I moved here. I never saw a corpse laid out on the sidewalk with a bullet through the skull until I came here. This is not the movies, but you take it in your stride. That's a terrible thing. After a while you develop a blasé streak as well as a sixth sense about where not to go. There's no hiding from danger: famous or anonymous, bodyguard or no bodyguard, you've still got to walk down the street – and nobody is immune. Look at John Lennon.'

But the city with a brash exterior has a warm heart – just like its people. New Yorkers, both native and immigrant, have a bullet-proof attitude. They *expect* to be ripped off or knocked about in some way, and are grateful when they get through another day un-scathed. That's the personality of the city. And, says Cory, to a teenage girl with stars in her eyes there's nowhere like it. 'The pace is so fast, you have to try harder at everything just to keep up. But it's a place where you can be whoever you want to be, however weird or wonderful. Nothing is unusual here, and nobody is ever shocked.'

Fashion Avenue, NYC, the main artery of the industry, is one of the least stylish strips of Manhattan. On the designers the irony is not lost, especially as they swish their well-dressed way through the busy brass revolving doors of No. 550 at around noon to be whisked to more salubrious addresses uptown for lunch. No. 550 Fashion Avenue is a Gothic tower housing the headquarters of most of America's top designers. It rises above a grime-encrusted, sleazy district groaning with doughnut bars and discount stores. Here dwell the choosers among the beggars, the Oscar de la Rentas, Donna Karans, Ralph Laurens, Bob Mackies and Bill Blasses who call the fashion industry shots. Eager young mannequins lucky enough to be chosen as house models feel a *frisson* of excitement every time they step into its brass lifts. House model today, Supermodel tomorrow – who knows? Naomi and every other New York model worth her salt substitute is as familiar with this address as she is with her own apartment.

Naomi's first year in New York was an endless and exhausting round of Go-Sees, Castings, Options, Provisionals, Tentatives, Confirmations and Shoots – not to mention the foreign assignments. The model agency jargon alone can be blinding during those heady early days, but a new model has to get the hang of it – as well as every other aspect of the job – pretty damned quick if she is going to hold her own in the piranha pool.

Once she had become acclimatized, familiarized herself with her new neighbourhood and sussed the basics of simply getting about in New York, the first task Naomi faced was forging a good relationship with her bookers. These are the agency staffers responsible for getting a model work and for looking after her, and it is vital for a model to have them on her side.

'I just couldn't live without my bookers in each country!' confessed Naomi, whose personal bookers now include Carole White at Elite Premier in London, and Ann Veltri and Roe in New York. 'They are very important to me. An agency represents you and gives you advice, especially about money and accountants and managing your affairs and stuff. But your booker is your friend, and you work together and trust each other. They actually live part of your life with you and even *for* you during the years that you are modelling. You get very close to them – when I call up the agencies, I only want to speak to that one person, and that's *it!*'

The booker will send a model on Go-Sees – informal appointments with clients or photographers, who may see dozens of girls (and/or boys) before they find one who fits that particular bill. Castings are auditions or appointments for actual assignments. Options, Pencils, Provisionals and Tentatives are all possible assignments. A

Confirmation means you got the job. A model may be booked for editorial and advertorial work – fashion and beauty shoots for magazines and newspapers; runway or catwalk – modelling for designer shows in the fashion industry's capitals; various other forms of 'live' modelling, such as TV commercials, rock videos, exhibitions and demonstrations; and for mail order catalogue work.

A keen professional like Naomi quickly masters the basics. She maintains a high standard of personal hygiene, ensuring that her legs and underarms are regularly depilated to keep them free from hair, has regular manicures, pedicures and facials – you never know when you are going to need your hands and feet as well as your face for a photo shoot – and makes sure that her model bag contains all the tools of her trade, which she constantly checks and replenishes.

What *does* a model keep in that big bag of kit she constantly lugs around with her? Fairly mundane stuff, truth be told – but every bit of it vital, especially in the early days when the assignments can be quite humble and the model may even be called upon to do her own hair and make-up. There's the must-have diary, often in the form of a large leather Filofax, with big spaces for each day to fit all the assignments and social engagements. A book or magazine to read while waiting around. Spare underwear, G-strings, tights, two or three pairs of shoes to cover all eventualities, hair and make-up bag, a nail kit, hygiene requirements such as razor and toothbrush, and of course the thing they all cheekily refer to as 'Prince Charles's favourite toy': a box of Tampax. Last but not least, the true Supermodel will never leave home without her mobile phone!

The one thing she can't afford to cart around with her, at least to begin with, is attitude. 'It takes a lot more than just a pretty face and a great body to make it,' one booker told me. 'Personality is very important – almost more so than her looks. We tell our girls *don't* have an attitude, be sweet and nice as pie to everyone, and try not to look shy, as people often mistake this for standoffishness and it puts them off. Be confident and be yourself – this gives you an edge. You mustn't be scared of yourself – you mustn't be scared of *projecting*.

You must look like you've got something going on on the inside. You've got to be amenable – what you're hoping is that people are going to book you again and again and again. If you're easy and fun to work with, it makes everybody's job a breeze, and they are going to want you back.'

But how does a booker advise girls to hold their own in the presence of, say, unscrupulous photographers who may try and take advantage of particularly young and inexperienced girls? 'It is rarely a problem, but it can happen,' the booker admitted. 'It can be quite worrying to think that these girls of fifteen and sixteen are being thrown in at the deep end and expected to fend for themselves. We try to be extremely careful about who we send them to, and expect the girls to report back if they do have a problem. If we've heard that a guy has come on to the model – "Let's just try that shot on the bed. . . . Let's just close this door and turn down these lights" – we make a noise about it and we don't work with him again. We rely on the girls to tell us. It can get hairy at times, but most of the girls can stick up for themselves. Perhaps it's sad, but it's a fact of modelling life: they do grow up very, very quickly.'

Nobody ever said it was easy. But nobody ever heard Naomi Campbell complain. At least, not in the good old days. 'Not only was she totally professional right from the beginning, but what made her so great was that she had so much energy,' recalled one of Naomi's contemporaries. 'It was almost like, what is she *on*?! She was never tired, she was always bubbly – people just loved working with her. She was great to have around, everyone seemed to want to know her, and she was like a magnet. And people weren't even jealous of her or bitchy about her because of it – she was so much fun to have along. With Naomi, you always got the impression that she was completely determined. She *had* to be the best. You could definitely tell that her career was the most important thing in her life. There *was* a certain shyness about her back then which can be appealing, especially in someone so beautiful. It was almost like she'd worked on it – that it was deliberate, a little bit of an act.'

'She always moved so incredibly well,' another American model remembered. 'And she always wanted it – the fame, the money, the megastar boyfriend. She wanted it so bad. When a girl really wants it, it's like, "Move over, I'm doin' it!"'

New York's trendiest designer Anna Sui, who owns a Biba-style emporium in the city filled with her own gorgeous designs, is one of Naomi's best friends. She admires Naomi's individual and very personal look, and the fact that she has now effected a personal style and no longer automatically opts for the standard off-duty model uniform of Alaia jacket, leggings and shades, but is just as likely to be seen in a second-hand dress which she has customized in some way herself. Sui says: 'Naomi is so wonderful because she has her own style. She loves beautiful fabrics, and she's got a great eye. She likes antique clothes, thrift-store stuff – she appreciates the crafts-manship in the old clothing which is unusual in such a young model. And she's a lot of fun to go shopping with! We do it a lot! We go to a flea market – when we went to London we went shop-ping to Camden. She'd always one of the first out of all those girls to appreciate a new look, to go with it and really explore it. She's very innovative, not only as a model but as a woman.'

Move downtown in Manhattan and the blistered tarmac gives way to cobbles. Disused tenements and warehouses have metamor-phosed into chic loft apartments, restaurants, galleries and boutiques. This is where the world's trendiest models, including Naomi, and those who have a particular fondness for models and fashion editors, like Def Jam supremo Russell Simmons, live. Joe Major, a black American photographer, remembers Naomi as a wide-eyed downtown girl in those delirious early days. Major observed her as she took to the lifestyle like a mallard to a moat.

'She seemed so thrilled to be a part of it, it was cute to see,' he re-members. 'You'd spot her hanging out, wandering about the neigh-bourhood, sometimes doing her own shopping. She was once seen out buying a mop! Nobody owns property in Manhattan unless they are seriously rich, so when she got her first apartment, everyone knew she was making *big* money. She got this fabulous place, and then it stayed empty for months. She didn't have a clue what to put in it.

'In the end, an interior designer friend of mine helped her to design and decorate it, and pick out furniture and stuff. He travels – he's been to China and Africa, and he's got these huge Chinese vases and artefacts from all over. He's very flamboyant, and deals expensive stuff. That's who she called in. You know, all that money and she couldn't get the place together. It was like she just didn't have any sense of style. But you have to remember that she was still very young then, and all her money didn't suddenly buy her taste. You know, her home background was not that sophisticated. *Anyone* who had a million dollars to spend would call in a designer to help decorate. Besides, she could argue, she was always travelling – when did she have time to shop for furniture?'

Whatever her early sense of style, or lack of it, Major remembers how committed to the profession she was when she first arrived on the New York modelling scene. 'She was extremely conscientious, very health-conscious – she watched what she ate, she exercised, and she would get very strict with her girlfriends. They would all go out at night and Naomi would be the one concerned about getting home at a reasonable hour to get the requisite beauty sleep. You'd hear her telling the other models, "You know, you've gotta take care of your skin, you've gotta watch what you eat, you've gotta get your act together and sort your book out, you've got a Go-See tomorrow." I used to think, "Hey, she's *on* it!"

'This was when she was on the rise. Now that she's *there*, it's a slightly different story. She's been known to stay out all night, she smokes and drinks. You never see her with her own cigarettes, but always "borrowing" someone else's. I'd see her drink champagne – and Guinness. She used to have this real shy side – you'd have to direct her in a photo shoot until she got going. Now she poses, she pouts, she's *fabulous*! She's a pro. You don't tell her what to do any more – she tells *you*. She'll get a little picky about lighting and stuff. She calls the shots. She'll show up late and be inconsiderate because she *can*. She's a superstar – you come to expect it from them.

'But if you look at the bare necessities, she's all there. Her skin is basically good – it'll break out here and there, but it's better than mine. She doesn't appear to have to diet – yet. That will come. She takes care of her hands and her nails are good – she has been known to wear extensions. As for her hair extensions, all that had to come off eventually. Because of all the stuff she put in her hair, it was never in the greatest condition. Even when she had those long extensions, it was an inch long against the scalp in parts where it had broken off. She's much better since she dropped the weaves, the wigs and the wacky make-up and got back to a more natural look. She has a very natural beauty, and she should make the most of that. I see her out sometimes with Christy Turlington and they always look perfect. When you're in the spotlight like that you *have* to be image-conscious.'

Naomi stopped telling fashion and beauty interviewers about which were her favourite cosmetics, however, after she once mentioned that she used a Kiehl's New York Pharmacy skin treatment, and the fact was repeated in magazines and newspapers all over the world. It did wonders for Kiehl's sales, of course. But it didn't exactly do a lot for Naomi. She didn't have a cosmetics contract, after all – why should she be endorsing a company's products for nothing? She is today very secretive on the subject of preferred brands of make-up. If a company wants her to say so, they are going to have to pay. . . .

Embraced by New York's beautiful people, and warmly welcomed into their inner circles and VIP lounges, Naomi was not the gauche New Kid in Town for very long. Virtually overnight she was an Access All Areas gal, the toast of Manhattan's fashion business and the darling of the best-dressed jet-set. She had been transformed as if by magic wand from anonymous newcomer to the Next Big Thing – thanks largely to friends like Linda Evangelista, who dragged her along to all the right parties and introduced her to influential people. Joining the ranks of the rich and trendy, Naomi opted for a downtown private life just a few bullet-proof limo-lengths from all the favourite places – like Nell's nightclub and the Merc Bar down Murphy Street, with its wondrous rear wall made of interlocking antlers, and the *Café Tabac*, hangout of Sean Penn, Robert De Niro, Madonna, Herb Ritts, Roseanne Barr, Sandra Bernhard, designers like Todd Oldham, Marc Jacobs and Isaac Mizrahi, writers like Hal Rubenstein of the *New York Times*, and the Condé Nast set. It was Herb Ritts who gave Naomi the fabulous diamond bracelet she wore on television during an interview with chat show host Arsenio Hall, about which the outrageous interviewer enquired: 'When your bracelet has babies can I have one?'

Naomi also numbers respected lensman Steven Meisel among her closest friends, as well as Evangelista, Turlington, the androgynous, eyebrow-less model Kristen McMenamy, and pop star Simon le Bon's model wife Yasmin, whom she sees mostly in Europe. All insist that there is no cattiness on or off the catwalk when Naomi is around, that they all get on famously and any other suggestion is mere *merde*. And every one of Naomi's friends prefers the downtown lifestyle to the pretensions of Park Avenue.

Also downtown, another very close friend of Naomi's, multi-millionaire music mogul Russell Simmons, lives upstairs from Keith Richards in Cher's old triplex, complete with Caligula-style bath-tub big enough for two and a four-poster bed in which he has entertained many a mannequin. In the West Village the models all rub shoulders with painters, musicians, scribes, actors and photographers, and move from one trendy venue to the next: slaves to the rhythm, Sultanesses of Style, just a cellular phone bleep away from anyone who might need them. Hot models like Naomi and their entourage have nothing if not a go-go lifestyle. They socialize incessantly. They schmooze with all the right and some of the wrong poeple. In TriBeCa – the Triangle Below Canal Street and a bleak, trendy district which is home to Robert De Niro's film production empire – they eat at the actors' to-be-seen-in bar and grill.

In the Union Square Café on 16th Street they munch on banana tart and killer tuna burgers – except Naomi, who hates tuna almost as much as she detests coffee. Naomi and her English cronies will go for more modest nosh to Tea and Sympathy, a tiny restaurant on Greenwich Avenue opened by a Londoner two years ago which is actually a cross between an English tea shop, a working men's caff and a pub. Here they serve Shepherd's Pie, Welsh Rarebit, Lancashire Hot Pot, Treacle Pudding, and scones with clotted cream and jam. It is a place for solace and spiritual renewal, and where Naomi is often to be found feasting on a full greasy English breakfast: bacon, eggs, mushrooms, sausages, the lot, washed down with endless cups of tea.

This was the first place at which Naomi suggested we should meet – but that morning it was closed, and we wound up at the deli a few doors down, where she scoffed a cheese and mayonnaise on rye sandwich instead. And wherever she can, she'll drink rosemary tea – which most places tell her they don't do, until she informs them that it's just the stuff you cook with lamb plus hot water. She may not miss Streatham High Road much, but there are certain home comforts a girl cannot live without. Her favourite goat curry and rice she has to wait for until she returns to London to visit her grandmother. But the Marmite and Jacob's cream crackers, Paxo stuffing and Christmas puddings are always available at Peter Myers' English food store, Myers of Keswick on Hudson Street – a fact of which all New York's British community is aware.

'See, be seen, *make* the scene. Naomi has certainly figured out how to do that, better than any of them,' comments New York celebrity photographer Nick Elgar, who has been known to attend four or five parties in uptown Manhattan in one night, and has occasionally seen Naomi at all of them. In the early days, at least, she'd arrive with her model girlfriends. Famous boyfriends, at that stage in the game, featured way, way down on Naomi's to-do list. It was only a matter of time. In the meantime, there was serious work to be done.

By August 1988, when she was still only eighteen, Naomi had appeared on the cover of British *Vogue* and had become the first-ever black cover girl for French *Vogue*. The following year she was featured in the September issue of Anna Wintour's American *Vogue* – traditionally, the most important issue of the year for the world's most influential fashion magazine. By the end of 1989 she was reckoned to have banked her first million, had appeared in three episodes of American TV's hugely popular *Cosby Show* with Bill Cosby, and was getting more modelling assignments than there are days in the year. *Everyone* wanted her – at *any* price, and she could name it.

She was also beginning to be more, much more, than just a model. See, be seen, make the scene, as Nick Elgar said: 'There she was at all the important parties – love her! – making friends with the ones who count, dressed up in chic to-die-for numbers by her designer friends Alaia and Rifat Ozbek. You couldn't help but notice her – she was *everywhere*. Her name began to appear alongside her picture – a real accolade for any model – as in 'Naomi Campbell wears. . . .'

And yet she did not take to sitting on her laurels, to wallowing in her success. There she was, still giving it all she'd got in acting, dance and voice classes whenever she found the time. It might have been easy to hang out with her friends every night, enjoying her money, her face, the Supermodel lifestyle and all its attendant perks, but there was work to be done. Naomi kept on swallowing her fistful of vitamin pills each morning, and applied herself to the various facets of her profession as if her life depended on it. There was still a long way to go. . . .

It was in May 1991 that Naomi knew for sure she had arrived. Not only did Madonna herself, in a scene-stealing tight black frock, show up to her model friend's twenty-first birthday party held at Laura Belle's elegant Manhattan supper club – but American *Vogue* devoted a whole page to the event, also attended by Diana Ross's model daughter Tracey. Noami, cute as apple pie in a low-cut gingham sun-dress revealing an inviting slice of bosom, looked pleased as Punch and Judy put together. No De Niro? No Tyson? *Well!* Not what you could call a star-studded night, then! Far from it, actually. As Joe Major, who photographed the event, pointed out: 'Madonna and Naomi at the same party is *more* than enough. . . .'

In September 1991 Naomi appeared on the front cover of *Time International* magazine, which carried a feature entitled 'Supermodels: Beauty and the Bucks'. In the piece, which hailed today's mannequins as more important than Hollywood movie stars, Naomi was the only model to warrant a full-page article just about her. Headlined 'A Celebrity's Celebrity', the piece compared her with Elizabeth Taylor and Madonna. The next month, she was interviewed live on British television on *Wogan*. Who'd ever heard of such a thing? Who cared? The whole world, in fact. For both of these achievements served to confirm Naomi Campbell's status as the most talked-about Supermodel on earth.

And here began the backlash. You are not allowed to have it all for long without starting the repayments. Here began the alleged rows and the tantrums. The rumours of bad behaviour, lateness, the no-shows, upon which the British and American tabloid press fell with glee. Build 'em up, knock 'em down, when was it different? Even the comics had to have their say, and Naomi suddenly found herself the butt of some not always good-natured humour. . . .

At a downtown comedy club tucked away along a side street close to where Second Avenue drops into Chrystie on Manhattan's Lower East Side, they are taking bucks on the door for the last performance. Seconds out, and the queue still stretches the length of the block. Inside the dive, a cigarette haze you could slice forms a screen between punters and brickwork. Fried food is passed around in baskets, beer in bottles, and a woman who wants a dry white spritzer watches a jaded waitress answer 'Yay' by rolling her eyes towards heaven.

'Any Irish in here tonight? Got any visitors in from the Emerald Isle among us this fine evening?' whines the MC, an ample, Medusa-haired female with a magenta gash for a gob, into her mike. The pianist on a battered upright slides into 'Danny Boy'. There follows a predictable string of mildly spiteful Irish gags in place of the standard Polish, and a rasp of laughter wafts towards the stage.

'Got any English gents or ladies in our midst this bitch of a ball-freezing night?' enquires the comic, revving up.

If there *are* any, none of us raises a thumb.

'Pity! I know you're out there with your personality defects! It's *your* dusky daughter we're gonna talk about here, right? . . . Naomi Campbell. Say it Nay-OH-Mi. NayOhMiGOD! I mean, the girl is so darned big here now, we pick up on every little sandwich that she *eats*. *Please*! She is a black comedy all by herself, and I don't mean to sound racist here – after all, I *am* Jewish. Hooker's body. Virgin's eyes. We're not talking Richard Branson, honey, *no*. But those *lips*! *Jeez*, were those lips made in heaven or where? They are *child*-bearing lips, please forgive me. Get her in a clinch with Mick Jagger and you'd never prise those suckers a-*part*!

'What has she *got*? You're asking *me*! Jealous? I just hate the bitch. Legs all the way to Supermodel heaven – you can kiss my ass if you can *reach*. And a butt tighter than a G-string on a Sumo wrestler. . . . Describe Naomi in terms of *food*, do I hear someone say? Okay – she's a sweet-and-sour something. Or a soft-shell crab . . . one that *name*-drops. She gets up to dance in some club, she's boasting, "Michael Jackson gave me these steps! Mm-Mm-MMMMM!" And I'm going, "Hell, I'll bet he was glad to be rid of them. . . ."'

Even the newspapers wanted a piece of that tight ass, the pound of flesh they felt they were due. Even now, they were waiting in the wings with sharpened laptops. . . .

6

Bad, Bad, Bad, Bad Girl

If it was Naomi's immersion into trendy New York society which confirmed her status as a Supermodel, it was undoubtedly her relationships with some very high-profile men which consolidated the cross-over to mainstream superstar. Once she had basked a little in their brand of blinding limelight, there was no turning back.

Set up as one of the world's most desirable sex objects so early in her life, Naomi was to be pitied, not blamed, for handling it badly at times. She had, after all, to make all her mistakes in the full glare of the public eye – unlike most of us, who are at least afforded a little privacy in which to lick our wounds when things go wrong.

Even when you are trained, groomed and fully prepared for stardom, and you want it more than anything in the world, nothing can quite prepare you for its devastating effect on your personal life – even when, like Naomi, you have all but designed your personal life to match your celebrity status. It hits you head-on like a runaway express train. You either hang on for dear life and go along for the ride, or you hit back. Naomi's main mistake since her rise to fame is that, at times, she has tried to have the best of all worlds and do both. It has taken her a long time to realize that the media are as great a force to be reckoned with as she is, and there is only one way to beat them: join in. Treat them with respect, and in return you will be afforded some. If you're lucky, they might even like you.

Part of the problem for celebrity models is that they do not have managers; they tend to manage themselves. Their agencies and their bookers take care of their professional assignments and advise on business affairs such as investing their money and paying taxes. A model as big as Naomi sometimes has a PA, spokesperson or a

Girl Friday – Naomi's have included the substantial Cassie Swain, with whom she has come to blows on the odd occasion, and a sweet assistant called Jade – to help organize her life. But when it comes to the big decisions there is no one to tell them what to do. A model relies on her own judgement, or sometimes that of a husband, boyfriend or parent, as in the case of Tyra Banks and her manager-mother, Caroline Jones.

It is one of the reasons that most models marry at a very young age: not only are they getting the security of a loving partner, but also someone to direct them through life. When Linda Evangelista married Elite's Paris model agency boss Gerald Marie, she was getting the whole secure lot in one package. Little wonder that the marriage eventually foundered and she took off with a glamorous and headstrong actor.

The more famous Naomi has grown year by year, the bigger her entourage has become. It is perhaps an indication of her inherent insecurity that she cannot quite concede control to one person. As we have seen, it is not usual for models to have personal managers. But for a girl like Naomi who is going in so many different directions at once, she of all models really needs one. With so many people on hand to advise her, offer their two penn'orth and dip in their oar, it is little wonder that things get confusing at times. Such advice is often conflicting; there are the inevitable emotional and political problems between those close to her; and meanwhile Naomi is the fragile Brown Girl in the Ring hardly knowing which way to turn or what to do for the best. It was one of the reasons why I encountered extraordinary difficulties when I set out to write this book. There being no consensus of opinion about whether or not the book would be good for Naomi – some secretly thought it *was*, but didn't dare tell her so – it was perhaps to be expected that she would be wary of what might or might not be on the cards.

Her problems are perhaps hard for those outside her world to understand. Here she is, a beautiful and glamorous millionairess with a string of famous boyfriends to her name and the world at her feet. How could her life possibly be difficult? And yet it *is*. For every Supermodel 'up' there is a 'down'. For all the joy there is sadness, or at least unbelievable frustration. The structure of her life is much like everyone else's, except on a far grander scale.

The modelling world is nothing if not stressful, if only because models do permanent battle with their weight, with skin problems and with tiredness. If a model shows up to a photo shoot sporting a pimple, it is a major problem and the model will feel like cutting her own throat. Paranoia will set in because she feels everybody is gossiping and hissing behind her back. The smallest hiccup in proceedings becomes an almost insurmountable disaster because everyone is permanently hungry, smoking too much and living on the raw edges of their nerves.

And the jet-set lifestyle always takes its toll. Businessmen who take transatlantic flights twice a month spend the rest of it trying to combat their jetlag as they struggle to meet deadlines. A Supermodel might make three or even more such flights in one *week*. Her schedules are crazy – she has to present herself for fittings of make-up sessions in far-flung cities at the crack of dawn. And not only that. A woman business executive is allowed to turn up for a board meeting a little puffy around the gills after deplaning the Red-Eye. As long as she's clean and smart, she's not there to be looked at. But a Supermodel has to look her best even though she is riddled with jetlag and has had perhaps no more than two or three hours' sleep a night for several weeks.

Her tremendous strength has always been Naomi's salvation, and has helped her hang on to the stardom she enjoys today. Those who are plucked from obscurity and become overnight sensations rarely handle the limelight as well as she has. Child singing star Lena Zavaroni turned from a fat little girl into a tragic, anorexic teenager. *ET* star Drew Barrymore was a drug and sex addict before she was thirteen. Judy Garland never came to terms with the pressures of fame, and was hooked on drink and drugs throughout her life until they wiped her out. Her daughter Liza Minnelli has herself been through the mill, hooked on alcohol and drugs and the survivor of several broken relationships. Elizabeth Taylor has been dogged by emotional and medical traumas since her teens. Julia Roberts has had one doomed romance after another, and married country singer Lyle Lovett in June 1993 seemingly on a whim.

Before we examine individually and in detail the relationships which have helped to make Naomi an international celebrity, it is worth pausing to reflect on why she has become so important to the media. Pictures sell newspapers. Naomi Campbell's photograph on the front page sells more than most. For this reason, editors and journalists will go to unimaginable lengths to find reasons why she should help them to do so. Candid shots of her regularly change hands for silly money, and anything which portrays her looking less than her perfect catwalk self is dynamite. The public likes nothing better than a celebrity with her make-up off or her knickers down. It just goes to prove what we always secretly suspected: that deep down they are no different, no better, than the rest of us. The paparazzo who gets a great candid shot of Naomi can virtually name his price. And even the grandest of gossip columnists will often bring himself to mention Naomi in his pages. Everyone is fascinated by her life and times. To be remembered, you've got to be so damned good, or so damned bad. . . .

As a sizeable proportion of the mediacracy would have it, Naomi perceived a gap in the Goody Two-Shoes Supermodel market for a black sheep – and deliberately set about wedging herself firmly into it before anybody else got a look in. The apocryphal story has her gazing upon the gorgeous faces and 'Nice Girls Don't' lifestyles of Cindy, Yasmin, Christy and Linda and thinking: '*Wait* a minute. This is all too squeaky clean for words, I'm outta here, I'm off to be a bad girl. . . .'

Having investigated this further, I find that there is very little truth in the theory. But if she *did* calculate the move, actually launching herself in hot blood as the Black Sheep of Supermodels, she'd be even smarter than we know. And if, more likely, this angle of her image was purely accidental, then bravo anyway. In setting herself up or otherwise as Naughty Naomi the Bitch from Hell, the niche she has claimed for herself is unique. For one thing, no one else *wants* it. But for another it sets her apart from the line-up in a category of one, so there is no choice but to look at her.

Let the girlies take their vitamins, spend cosy evenings grilling fish in lime and honey, share a cautious occasional half-glass of Zinfandel with husband or loving live-in, and get an early night. They're welcome to it. Naomi, meanwhile, is in training for that longed-for day in the not too distant future when she launches herself on the rock world as a singer. . . .

From this viewpoint, it all adds up. Good gals take a beautiful picture and look pretty on the page, but bad gals make scintillating copy. Mention the name 'Naomi Campbell' and every news editor in the land is all ears. STREET BRAWLER NAOMI . . . SEX KITTEN IN CAT FIGHT . . . NAOMI: BEAUTY AND THE BEAST . . . NAOMI FLIES IN WITH A JET-STREAM OF ABUSE . . . CATFIGHT ON THE CATWALK: these are the banner headlines we have come to associate with her name. They are not pretty stories, but they all add to her 'Streatham Stray Cat' image.

It was in May 1992 that the storm broke over Naomi's so-called scrap with an actress over someone else's husband. 'Supermodel Naomi Campbell wrestled with her best friend in a pavement catfight over a married man,' reported Ivor Key from New York in the *Daily Express* on 20 May 1992.

> 'She grabbed former *Dynasty* star Troy Beyer by the hair, called her "a whore" and started brawling outside a nightclub,' said onlookers. The fight came during celebrations for Naomi's 22nd birthday just before she was due to leave New York and return home to see her mother in London. Guests, who included Grace Jones and rock star Lennie Kravitz, said the fight started because each thought the other was paying too much attention to American TV star Damon Wayans.

In America, supermarket tabloid the *Star* reported the same story on 2 June:

Friendship turned to fisticuffs for Supermodel Naomi Campbell and former Dynasty star Troy Beyer outside New York City's Roxy disco over the attentions of *In Living Color*'s very married Damon Wayans. . . . 'Naomi is very obsessive of her friendship with Troy', says one friend. The evening started at the TriBeCa Grill . . . where 26-year-old Troy was throwing a 22nd birthday party for Naomi. The revelers moved over to the Roxy where the fight erupted. Tempers remained on the boil even inside the club where, according to a witness, petulant Naomi threw a drink across the room. Meanwhile, while Troy was off dancing, 31-year-old Damon, whose wife Lisa and four children were back home in Los Angeles, tried to calm Naomi.

Troy Beyer's manager, Sizanne Schacter, dismissed the fight as 'a mishap between two "sisters" who love each other and are still friends'. But when I tackled her about it face-to-face, Naomi told me: 'It *wasn't* my birthday. I didn't smash Troy in the face, and she's *not* a friend of mine – she's definitely not my *best* friend! I know her, I like her. I don't really want to comment on it, but I *did* hit her. There were two reasons. I'm not a tit-for-tat peson, and I don't want to say what they were. She said things – they were really damaging to me – about my feelings for other people and about my friends. I thought it was wrong. When you're friends with someone and you let them into your life and let them wear your clothes, try to look after them and support them, and they do things to betray you, it hurts. Anyone would react.

'Also, they put in the story that it was over a guy. It wasn't. I wouldn't fight over *any* guy – none of them is worth it! I don't know the guy in question. I met him one time in my life and said, "Hi, how are you?" That also was a lie. But to say she was my best friend was the worst thing. In this life you can count your best friends on one hand if you're lucky.'

Mutual friends of the pair have since commented privately that such an encounter was nothing to be surprised about. Rivalry, they say, always existed between the two girls, who have both appeared in videos for Prince and Michael Jackson.

Another press report had her whacking her mother on the dance floor of Sharks nightclub. This Naomi also denies. 'I never hit my mother on a dance floor in my life!' she told me. 'My mother hit *me*. She had every right to hit me – I said something that she didn't like. She doesn't like me swearing, and I think I used a word she hates, and she hit me. I'm her daughter, she's my mother, and no one will come between a daughter and a mother. She has every right to do whatever she likes. And by the way I've never even been in a nightclub with my mother – that's total invention.'

Nevertheless, I told her, she has a reputation now, right or wrong, for being aggressive. People say that she fights like a man, packs a punch like a prizefighter.

'Who would *know* that?' she snapped. 'I don't punch people! It's not something I do. That's the first time I can remember hitting someone, and now it's like I'm fighting every day.'

I have to say that she didn't seem very aggressive to me. But was she on her best behaviour for our meeting?

There are multiple facets to every story. Photographer Joe Major, who has often moved in Naomi's circle, knows a different side of her completely. Speaking over lunch at chic Lola's Bar, Joe revealed: 'She *is* a volatile girl, she's very up and down. I remember at the premiere of Madonna's film *Truth or Dare*, Naomi wore a really silly outfit. She was dressed up like a little girl – the hair, the beads. She looked really dippy. And she was getting into the limo with Steven Meisel and behaving like an absolute child, a real brat.

'I knew an artist, a Spanish illustrator, he's done a lot of stuff with Elite, he's known Naomi a while. One day the two of them had a fight. And she fights, believe me. You say something about her man, for example, she gets very angry and protective. You insult her and watch out. It's not true to say she doesn't fight with her closest friends. She *does*. Anyway, these two had a fight in an elevator. She hit him, and he hit her back. She punches like a man. She's strong, aggressive, she hits back. She feels free to slug, as they say, and she did. She slugged him right in the face. So he was fighting

her back, and he tore a piece of her hair out. She had these hair extensions at the time, and he ripped the back right out. She went
berserk.

'Those two fought in the street once, too. It's something she
does. She's *from* the streets. She never blew up at me, but I wouldn't
encourage it either. She's a hot cookie. She's not cool. She's ex-
citable. She needs a lot of attention. She sort of has to be with
somebody, she always needs to have a man. She won't show up at
things by herself. She puts on that soft, breathy little-girl voice, but
don't be fooled by it.'

Misrepresented and damaged by press speculation, gossip and
pure invention she may well have been. But the one error of judgement guaranteed to compound her 'Bad Girl' image for the rest of
time, Naomi managed all by herself. In stripping naked for
Madonna and posing explicitly in the pop singer's porn picture
book *Sex*, Naomi made a very big mistake.

Errors of judgement – we all make them. Her business decisions,
like everyone else's, cannot always be perfect. But it is perhaps hard
to understand why a Supermodel so much in demand should have
taken part in such a dubious project. Nudity in itself is no big deal,
but *Sex* takes raw nakedness and sexual gratification to extremes.
Masquerading as a celebration of modern erotica, the spirally
bound, steel-covered volume is a very explicit book which some
might even call tacky.

Perhaps this association with Madonna, then the biggest star in
the world, was too great an invitation to resist. Naomi already enjoyed her own extremely high profile, but the glory reflected from
the ultimate Material Girl could surely do her no harm. Perhaps, as
Naomi has since protested, she didn't realize what the assignment
entailed until she got there, when it would have been too late, too
embarrassing and too expensive to pull out. Perhaps it *was* a fast,
crazy, chaotic shoot. Maybe she didn't realize just how wild it would
all look until she saw the finished product. The photographer,
Steven Meisel, is a very close friend of hers, so she would not have

questioned his judgement. It was, perhaps, just another example of Naomi's slightly misguided ambitiousness.

On Saturday, 30 January 1993, Naomi dashed from an all-day photo shoot at London's Metro Studios – where she had posed for *Marie Claire* magazine's April 1993 front cover, shot by Willie Camden – to appear as a special guest on Jonathan Ross's Channel 4 TV show *Saturday Zoo*. On air, she confessed to him that she desperately regretted having done the Madonna pictures, that she would never do such a thing again, and that she hadn't realized what was expected of her until she got there. When Ross quizzed her on why she regretted the assignemnt so deeply, she replied: 'Because it upset my friends and family. It upset my mother very much, and I would never do it again.'

Naomi had now set herself up as fair game for anything. It was only a matter of time before the newspapers would start hinting that she is set to show us the only part of her anatomy we haven't yet glimpsed.

'No pink to show' is the hilariously coy phrase they use on the picture desks of certain girlie magazines when vetting shots for their raunchy layouts. But, it would seem, Naomi is prepared to show even that. 'NAOMI TO BARE ALL FOR £350,000,' blared the *Daily Mirror* on 30 March 1993. 'Supermodel Naomi Campbell is set to pick up £350,000 . . . by baring all for a *Playboy* centrefold,' reported Allan Hall from New York. He went on:

> She has already done a sizzling photo session for the magazine. Her personal assistant last night did not deny that the British-born beauty is keen to finalise the deal. And a *Playboy* spokeswoman said revealingly: 'We don't confirm anything until right before publication. Let's just say that if she does do it, she will be in good company: with Cindy Crawford, Stephanie Seymour and Rachael Williams'. All three are catwalk queens whose careers soared when they were featured naked in the magazine.

But Elizabeth Norris at the Playboy Enterprises Headquarters in

Chicago admitted: 'I don't know if she's doing it. Even if I *did* know I wouldn't say anything about an upcoming issue. We never publicise what's to be featured in a future issue before publication. We cannot confirm or deny whether she is appearing for us.'

But is she the sort of model they would *like* to feature in the magazine?

'I think you could say that,' conceded Ms Norris. 'Let's just say that there are things happening down the line that she *might* be included in, but at this point we have no comment to make either way. There are rumours which neither *Playboy* nor Naomi Campbell would confirm, is the only thing that's true at this point.'

But the *Daily Express*'s fashion writer Ann Chubb reported in a special Supermodels pull-out supplement to that newspaper on 19 April 1993: 'New York is awash with rumours that Naomi is going to do a centre spread for *Playboy* – even that she's already been photographed for one. She hotly denies this. "I will never do *Playboy*,"' Miss Chubb quotes Naomi as having told her.

> 'I'm not interested. Everyone is in control of their body and if they want to do it, that's fine. I just don't think it's me somehow. I didn't feel very comfortable about doing the Madonna book, to be honest. I did it because the photographer Steven Meisel is a really good friend of mine. And I didn't know what I was going to be doing until I got there, but I couldn't be unprofessional and refuse.'

Today, she would probably do just that.

It would be all too easy to condemn the British tabloids for Naomi's controversial media profile. In fact, the New York hawks have made a considerable contribution to her infamy. Much of what we read in our papers about Naomi actually originated in New York. It is because she has made that city her home and operates from there as the chic girl-about-globe.

But a celebrity's real press enemies in America are the supermarket rags – 'The 'Bloids', as controversial comedienne Sandra

Bernhard refers to them. These are the mass-circulation, muck-raking weeklies such as the *National Enquirer, Star* and *Globe*, whose British editor, Wendy Henry, is a former editor of the *News of the World*. Peddling as news the weird, the wonderful and the down-right sordid – alien babies from outer space, Wolf-Men, Liz Taylor's latest wonder-diet, the sensational secrets behind Jacko's skin com-plaint – they represent the dregs of gutter journalism. Yet millions of Americans are addicted to them, snatching them up with the shopping at the check-out. And they appear to have a network of contacts second to none, judging by the depths to which their reve-lations sometimes sink.

Tit-bits on Naomi's personal life and in particular her men feature regularly. The plus side is that such exposure has only served to make her a household name coast-to-coast. Less Supermodel, more super*market* model, it would seem. But can she really com-plain – as long as they spell her name right?

Actually, she can. If you have gone to great lengths to conceal secrets about your personal life which might injure your reputation if ever they came to light, you can be sure the Bloids will one day uncover them. It is only a matter of time, of making someone an offer they can't refuse. Robert Redford's character John Gage in the blockbuster movie *Indecent Proposal* was nearly right when he told Demi Moore that anyone can be bought. When the price is right, almost everyone comes on down.

Her loveliness goes on and on. But every now and then Naomi will pull a stroke which leaves the fashion world gasping, and has news editors holding the front page. Is there no limit to her ruthlessness? Or does she simply feel that, having slogged out her guts to be what she is today – the world's top black model – she is not about to re-linquish her crown to, nor be upstaged by, a copycat upstart?

Back in March 1993, incensed by gossip within the business that Californian teenager Tyra Banks was imitating her style and trying to steal her thunder, Naomi wielded her considerable power and had her nineteen-year-old adversary dropped from Karl Lagerfeld's show for Chanel in Paris. 'If she appears, I don't,' she reportedly told Lagerfeld. The designer, who is said to adore Naomi, complied; Tyra was fired; and once again Naomi emerged the victor. Further proof, as if it were needed, that the girl is a dab-hand at getting her own way.

Tyra Banks was to prove a threat that would not go quietly, however. When she was featured in *Sports Illustrated*'s annual swimsuit issue, sales of the magazine soared to 10 million copies. In April 1993 she made fashion history by becoming the first black model to appear in designer Ralph Lauren's advertising campaign. And, as if this were not enough, offers for lucrative cosmetics contracts that had always eluded Naomi started to flood Tyra's way.

'This is an industry in which imitation can be very costly,' one American magazine writer told me. 'To date, Naomi has tended to treat Tyra more like a protégée than a rival. She came on like the big sister, even shared her vitamin pills with Tyra on a shoot for *Vogue* here that they did together, and started to offer her career tips.

'But to be honest, Tyra has a nicer nature deep down. And so far she's not a prima donna. She's sweet, she's not too grand to turn up on time to shoots or for fittings. More and more people were talking about Tyra and comparing her to Naomi, and bitchy types couldn't resist reporting back to Naomi and winding her up. "She's copying your hair . . . she's copying your clothes . . . she's practising your walk" – this and that.

'Last November, a number of the designers here used Tyra in their shows. And it did seem that Naomi was constantly being upstaged by her. Everyone appeared to be looking to see what Tyra would do next, and Naomi, by contrast, seemed to lack her usual sparkle. Cindy Crawford actually came right out and said Tyra's was "the best performance of the season. She just commands attention," she said.'

On 7 March 1993 the *Mail on Sunday* reported: 'At the Anne

Klein Show [in New York], Naomi is supposed to have spotted the show-stopper – a clingy black crochet tube dress – hanging on her rival's rail. When she expressed her chagrin, the designer allowed her to try it on and then inflicted the ultimate humiliation by deciding it looked better on Tyra.'

Tyra Banks denies this, as you might expect. In the fashion world, gossip need not be true as long as it's juicy. 'Out of the top ten girls, there is Naomi,' said Tyra generously when quizzed about her more senior rival. 'In the top twenty there's still only Naomi. This industry is pitting black models against black models. I want to see more than one top black model. I don't want to be *the* next one. I want to be *one* of the next.'

While the fashion world could be growing tired of Naomi's petulance, most commentators agree that Tyra Banks is refreshingly professional. 'I regard that as the ultimate compliment,' Tyra bubbles. 'When I walk down the runway I'm thinking about how much I love to entertain and rock the crowd. But I'm also thinking: "Buy this dress!"' she admits.

Discovered in 1991, Tyra had done some modelling work part-time while still attending high school in Los Angeles. Offered places at five universities, she chose instead to take a sabbatical and signed with Naomi's own modelling agency, Elite. Her rise was spectacular in an industry which cannot accommodate as many black girls as white. What's more, her face was hauntingly reminiscent of Naomi's when she first started out: fresh, innocent, big baby eyes that were still seeing things for the first time.

'This rivalry has been blown out of all proportion,' comments the London *Evening Standard*'s marvellously outspoken fashion writer Lowri Turner. 'If you think back to the last season, there was Beverley Peel, Tyra, Naomi – there were the three of them and they were used an awful lot. This season Tyra was used hardly at all. I thought that, after the last season when she did so well, she would have replaced Naomi, but she didn't. It's partly because black isn't fashionable at the moment – it's all waify and thin and white. It's all Kate

Moss. So black girls have got a bit of a problem because they're more muscular, they've got more attitude, and the designers don't want attitude at the moment, they want drippy. . . .'

On 4 April 1993, Richard Johnson reported in the *New York Daily News*: 'Naomi Campbell won another skirmish in her fashion feud against rookie model Tyra at the Isaac Mizrahi show.' And photographer Wendy Jordan, who was at the show which was also attended by actress Ellen Barkin with Steven Meisel, Liza Minnelli, Roseanne Barr and Sandra Bernhard, who were commenting on the event together for television, added: 'It was Naomi's night all right. She had her mother there and a whole posse of friends, completely outnumbering Tyra's. The look on Tyra's face! It was as if she just wanted to cry. Naomi was then surrounded by her best friends Christy Turlington, Linda Evangelista and Kristen McMenamy as they posed for pictures after the show. But by the time we got back-stage, Tyra was long gone.'

When the *New York Times* interviewed Naomi on 11 April 1993, quizzing her about the rivalry between herself and Tyra, she told them: 'I don't want to talk about it. I haven't a thing to say.' The wisest comment, perhaps, in view of the fact that Tyra Banks had just pulled out of her contract with Elite and gone off to find a new agency. Shortly afterwards she signed with Mark McCormack's modelling division at IMG.

'Tyra is no longer with Elite,' confirmed flamboyant and eccentric agency boss Johnny Casablancas. 'And it's true, she does blame us for not taking a stand. We lost her because we would not take sides in all this. She does not want to be at the same agency as Naomi. They are two beautiful models and a lot of people made sure they hated each other. We should have sat down with them both a long time ago and talked it out. Even though Naomi is an explosive young lady, we could also see her point of view.'

He admitted that Tyra's manager, her mother Caroline Jones, was extremely upset by the slights against Tyra which Naomi is alleged to have made. Perhaps, being her mother, she took the matter more personally than would the usual handler. Casablancas would only say that her involvement 'made things a little more complicated'. And, he added sadly: 'It's very unfortunate. People were fuelling things, antagonizing Naomi. It was very unpleasant to be caught in the middle. I do think Tyra is a great beauty with a great career ahead of her. For me, this was a no-win situation.'

You win some, you win some. Naomi must be blessed. She has the magic touch, a knack for turning even painful and embarrassing experiences to her advantage and for milking a situation for all it is worth.

'There's news, and there is news. I couldn't believe it when I saw it on *News at Ten*,' laughed Lowri Turner in reference to Naomi's 'Fall from Grace' on the Paris catwalk, when she famously fell off her Vivienne Westwood purple platforms and crashed agonizingly on to her bottom.

'Girls are *always* falling down!' added Lowri, who had witnessed the tumble live in Paris. 'But this was big-time news partly because it was Naomi Campbell, partly because it involved a British designer – the name Vivienne Westwood actually registers with news editors here because she was an infamous punk, British Designer of the Year, etc. Also, they just happened to have cameras there. At most of the shows abroad, there wouldn't necessarily be a British news crew. All these factors contrived to make it big, big news. I was amazed! But this was also a chance for news editors to prove how ridiculous platform shoes are – they all hate them.

'Falling down is what a model fears most. But if she can carry off a fall with a smile, then she usually gets a round of applause. In many ways, they should all fall down once a season, because then everybody would really like them and say, "Oh, well, she's only human!"'

At least Naomi had the grace to laugh.

Sticks and stones. There is one way not to be hurt by bad press, and that is not to read it. Naomi claims she never does. 'I don't read the papers anywhere in the world,' she told me. 'That's my self-protection device.' And that's not to say she doesn't mind what they say. 'I *do* mind,' she admitted. 'I'm only human like everybody else. But when it's not true, there's nothing I can do to change it. So I just ignore it.'

Ignoring it has its perils. It is as if Naomi took a leaf out of Michael Jackson's book long before she ever got to co-star in his video. He is concrete proof that the more elusive you are, the more they want you. The less you tell about your private life, the more they will exaggerate and invent, until you, the celebrity, acquire by default an alter ego far more fascinating and compelling than little old you could ever manage by yourself. Which does the media job nicely without you ever having to lift a finger.

Others insist that, with Naomi, the boot's on the other foot. Says photographer Terry O'Neill, who has taken pictures of so many celebrities that he has become one himself: 'She has this incredible knack of being in the right place at the right time. It's remarkable the way she does it – she never ceases to amaze me. Don't underestimate her – she's a very astute girl for her age, she's really very bright. She has got where she is as much on wits and guts as she has on her looks.'

If things get too bad she could always sue. Then again, as Cher once said to me, there are so many lies written about *her* that she could spend every day of her life engaged in litigation. Exaggeration, of course, is a way of life in showbiz, and it is often impossible to separate the facts from the fiction, the reality from the myth. Naomi is the sum total of her own ambition, of media hype, rumour, gossip and speculation. The facts are often so dull as to be not worth bothering about.

Nevertheless, when you hit the top of the fame tree it is usual to try to manage and control your media image – or to hire someone to do it for you. The industry cheered when Naomi hired New York top gun Susan Blond, a no-nonsense woman with an excellent reputation as a publicist. She of all people could consolidate Naomi's image. A publicist's brief, in brief, is to get a client into the papers as much as possible while he or she is trying to build up a profile – then keep them *out* of the papers as much as possible, except on account of their professional activities, once they have made it. When Naomi unfathomably parted company with Susan Blond after the most abbreviated relationship, she once again found herself at the mercy of a gaggle of players with her best interests at heart.

Subsequent publicists have perhaps not been as experienced as Naomi needs. Thus she sometimes misses the point about how to handle her own image. While Carole White and the rest of the team at Elite Premier in London are professional, reasonable, reliable and have made a pretty good job of this, it is not really their *job* to deal with the press. Until now, Naomi has had no official publicist in Britain.

Does Naomi really believe that the British press have it in for her? 'I don't know,' she told me. 'I expected it in some ways, I guess. People in Britain seem to have this peculiar attitude towards people who have made something of their lives. They build them up and then they knock them down. It's something I knew was going to happen one day. I'm not letting it affect me, though.'

It is the allegations of unprofessionalism, of no-shows and persistently poor time-keeping that hurt her the most. 'You know what?' she said to me. 'I'll tell you the problem. Agents. Time differences. New York. London. Paris. Barcelona. Milan. Los Angeles. They call me at seven in the morning, start giving me all the options, who wants me, where I have to be. . . . ' She quotes the Concorde timetable from memory as if she were talking commuter trains.

'Which is *great*, of course. I'm working – I'm not complaining. But you're talking, talking, talking on the phone, and suddenly it's nine o'clock. And by the time you are out of the door and have got to your first job, it is ten o'clock and you are late. I always say I am *really* sorry, I will stay late, as long as it takes, make up the time. I always stay until the job is done. Everybody ends up happy. But now I'm a little more organized. I have a girl, Jade, who works with me, takes the phone calls, arranges my timetable.

'I have *never* not shown up at all – that is a very unfair accusation. I was never even booked to do the Calvin Klein show they say I missed. They are talking about another model. Her mistake has given *me* this terrible reputation. Neither did I ever say that I never get out of bed for less than $15,000 a day. I would *never* say that. Another model said that and I have borne the brunt of it all this time. No, I don't want to say who said it [it is widely assumed to be Linda Evangelista at the going rate of £10,000 per day] because I don't think she said it in a negative way. But it's unforgiveable. It's pompous and conceited. I think, you know, in all this there could be a racial problem. Why are they saying *I'm* the one, not her? She'll not turn up for three *days* and still keep her advertising contract. They'll take that behaviour from her. All I am is a little late. The difference, to me, is black and white.'

She should complain. Whatever else they said about her, at least they spelt her name right. And once they started linking it to some of the world's most eligible men, Naomi's superstar status was confirmed. The other Supermodels could only ponder where they went wrong. . . .

7

Is She Really Going Out With Him?

Rule number one in the avoidance of Kiss and Tell is to choose partners who are at least as famous as yourself. That way, you can be sure they won't go running to tabloid newspapers demanding fat cheques for sexy revelations about what went on and what went wrong. It is a lesson that Naomi learned very early on. It also made her all the more attractive to the celebrities who would court her. She was never likely to spill any beans, because she had just as much to lose as they did.

This is the reason why precious little is known about the ins and outs of her so-called fairytale romances with the stars. When quizzed on the subject in interviews, she'll rarely give more than a sweet but firm 'No comment'. And her men have always been at least as enigmatic as she is. Thus has the irresistible mythology evolved about Naomi and Mike Tyson, Naomi and Robert De Niro, Naomi and Sylvester Stallone, Naomi and Eric Clapton. Plenty of others showed more than a passing interest, including Eddie Murphy – who signed her programme at a New York Aids benefit with the word 'Heaven' and an arrow pointing to his home phone number; *and* Viscount Linley – who pleaded with Naomi to be his tourist guide around New York City. It is unlikely that we will ever know what actually went on between them behind closed doors. Nevertheless, the kind of men she has been attracted to says much about her own personality and the things she fears are lacking in her life. There are, too, some fascinating parallels to be drawn between the men in question, which indicate what Naomi believes she needs from a partner, and the qualities she most admires in a man.

Not only have all her boyfriends been extremely famous, but each was at the pinnacle of his profession when she met him. All, except Mike Tyson, have been considerably older than Naomi; in the case of De Niro, Stallone and Clapton, old enough to be her father. The psycho-analysts I interviewed on the subject saw a clear need for a father substitute. This, however, was something that Naomi herself vehemently denied, denouncing the confusion of father-figure with lover as 'creepy'. Does she protest too much? One wonders.

All except U2 guitarist Adam Clayton – the only one who asked her to marry him – came from broken homes. All of them had strong and influential mothers or mother-figures, who had played a far more important part in their upbringing than their fathers. And all of them were suckers for a pretty face.

The prizefighting element which links Tyson with De Niro, through his portrayal of Jake La Motta, the *Raging Bull*, and with Stallone, through his alter ego Rocky, must be acknowledged here, since it suggests that Naomi is turned on by physically as well as socially powerful men. Is it so surprising? Naomi started out, after all, on the kind of backstreets where men do deals with their fists, and where brutal confrontation is a fact of life. The seedy underworld from which prizefighters tend to emerge had been familiar to her since childhood.

Naomi's blazing sexuality is her most powerful tool. Certainly in the case of Mike Tyson, it was so powerful that it almost got the better of him. When they met, he was the heavyweight champion of the world. If you are going to make a thing of celebrity boyfriends, he was not a bad place to start. Tyson was then twenty-one, the richest athlete in history but carrying a lot of baggage from a deeply deprived childhood. He had been born on 30 June 1966 in Bedford-Stuyvesant, a section of East New York through which it is advisable to travel by armoured car. Like Naomi's mother Valerie, Mike's unmarried mother, Lorna Tyson, had been abandoned by his father, Jimmy Kirkpatrick, before the baby was even born. Father and son never met.

Mike was raised on the desperate streets of Brownsville, went days without food and wore bits of cardboard in his shoes to patch the holes. His gentle and principled mother abhorred violence and did her best to teach her son the difference between right and wrong, but life in their neighbourhood was tough, and you had to hit back to survive. Lorna, overcome by the misery of their poverty-stricken existence, took to drink. Eventually it killed her.

Tormented as a child because of his lisp and high-pitched voice, Tyson developed his violent streak in self-defence. As a young teenager he began to hang with the hard men, mugging and stealing, and was often consigned to detention centres. At one such institution he met a former professional boxer who was to teach him the skills which would make him the world's most famous prize-fighter since Muhammad Ali. For Tyson, Ali, 'The Greatest', was the ultimate example of a black man making it in a white man's world, who had achieved wealth and power on his own terms without compromising himself or his values. It was an ideal to which both Tyson and Naomi related, and would attempt to make work for them also.

Taken on by legendary fight trainer Cus D'Amato at the age of fourteen, he was encouraged to develop not only as a fighter but as a man of the world. D'Amato isolated Tyson's primary motivation – fear – and trained him to deploy it positively in the ring. He encouraged Tyson's interest in literature, and gave him open access to his own considerable home library.

Tyson's professional career began in March 1985. Twenty months later he knocked out Trevor Berbick with blinding speed – their encounter lasted just five minutes and thirty-seven seconds – and was proclaimed heavyweight champion of the world. At just over twenty years of age, he was the youngest heavyweight champion in history.

The more successful he became, however, the unhappier he

grew. Lamenting the loss of his mother, he longed for someone with whom to share his success. He was inundated by offers from all kinds of women, but knew in his heart that they were attracted to him for all the wrong reasons.

'They don't want me, they want the cash', he once said. 'I look in the mirror every day, and I know I'm not Clark Gable. I wish I could find a girl who knew me when I was broke, and thought I was a nice guy.'

One insider close to Tyson said: 'When it comes down to it, he didn't care about looks. If he liked someone, he'd be with them whether they were attractive or not, white or black . . . He screwed around a lot, but I always felt what was inside someone counted to him.'

By virtue of his fame and wealth Tyson had been adopted by the black jet-set of New York – musicians and artists, designers, fashion types and fixers – and had begun to experience a world he could never have imagined on the streets of Brownsville. He was now the biggest-earning sports hero of all time, but he never truly came to terms with the magnitude of his wealth.

Former top model Beverly Johnson, the first black face to grace the cover of *Vogue*, remembered meeting Tyson one evening at Columbus, a late-late supper joint on Manhattan's Upper West Side where she was dining with a gaggle of pals. 'He was on the horizon and I knew about him because I knew about boxing, and I thought he was a sweet guy . . . we all became friends. He wanted to be introduced to that jet-set life in New York that I was very much a part of then, and everyone just fell in love with him.'

Tyson started running with the fashionable pack. Whoever was Who's Who in New York's black modelling world, Tyson was introduced to. The crowd would eat dinner at Mr Chow's, an exclusive Chinese restaurant, and hang out at Nell's, the elite nightspot.

'He was shy, very shy,' said Quentin Yearby, sleek black companion and colleague of lingerie designer Fernando Sanchez. 'But he was not a dumb boxer. His "Michael Jackson" voice, I found, as the French would say, *sympathique*. Here's a boxer who devastates people in the ring and he has this *tiny* little voice . . . he was like a teddy bear, a child . . . an ill-mannered child that needed some guidance. He needed to meet the right people.'

Tyson thought all his Christmases had come at once. He was suddenly meeting all these beautiful girls he had only seen before on the covers of glossy magazines. But he had a lot to learn before they would be totally at ease in his company. He had some gross habits which his new-found friends took pleasure in helping him to drop, such as the way he chewed his food, and the way he'd emerge for the evening dripping in vulgar quantities of gold jewellery. They showed him how to dress, where to go, what to say. He started attending the fashion shows, and was knocked out by what he saw. He was especially blown away by the new English girl on the block, Naomi Campbell.

They met one night at Quentin Yearby's birthday party, held at Fernando Sanchez' elegant Manhattan apartment. It was some occasion: sixty or so over-dressed guests, excess food and booze, pet parrots whizzing all over the place – chic madness to all the extremes.

Naomi was still fresh and young and naive, and *gorgeous*. Seventeen years old, recently in from London, and Supermodel stardom had yet to set in. But Tyson knew exactly who she was. He had seen her photographs everywhere, and he was itching to make contact with her. He pestered Yearby for an introduction, an idea which horrified Yearby. He told Tyson: 'She's a lady! You can't treat her like you treat all those other girls!'

When Naomi arrived at the bash with Linda Evangelista, Tyson, stiff in his dinner suit, was lurking behind the door. As she later reported, she had seen pictures of him . . . but she just wasn't prepared for his enormous size.

What was later to take place, or otherwise, between them that evening has been the subject of fierce debate ever since. But several guests who attended the party remember Tyson's relentless pursuit of Naomi as a cross between full-on flirtatiousness and blatant sexual harassment.

The couple spent most of the evening together on a leather settee in an upstairs lounge. 'She was flatly making eyes at him,' said one guest. Tyson, evidently, could barely contain his lust. From time to time a yelp for help was heard wafting from the third floor, and Naomi's girlfriends would dash to her assistance. Three or four times this happened. On his final desperate attempt Tyson wasn't taking no for an answer. 'We couldn't make him let go,' said a guest who had rushed to Naomi's aid. 'She was screaming and he was pressing her against the wall, her arms up in the air.'

In the end it was a pensioner who forced Tyson to desist. The late Sir Freddy Ayer, then seventy-seven and always thoroughly English in his approach, apparently stalked into the room, tapped Tyson on the back and commanded: 'Unhand that girl!'

Tyson is said to have spun round and snarled: 'Who in the hell are you?'

To which Ayer retorted: 'I am the most eminent philosopher of the twentieth century. Who in the hell are you?!'

Undeterred, Tyson later cornered Naomi in a downstairs bathroom from which her screams could clearly be heard. Her would-be rescuers hammered on the door, crying 'Open up!' – to no avail. 'We were yelling, "Mike, you've got to let her out – she's seventeen years old and she doesn't know what she's doing to you!"' recalled one.

Later, recalling that colourful birthday party, Yearby said of Naomi: 'Drama Queen to death!' To *death*! I don't think anything really happened, but she was very young, and Mike is very forceful.'

Remembering the occasion herself some time later, Naomi admitted that he was chasing her all over the apartment that night asking could he sit next to her, could he sit next to her, until finally she said okay, yes, he could. She was, she said, a little nervous of him: ' . . . He's so *big* and everything.' But she also insisted: 'He didn't hurt me in any way, ever, in our whole relationship.'

In fact, friends reported, the couple soon began seeing each other regularly and were an item, off and on, for about eighteen months. Members of Tyson's own entourage referred to their affair as 'one of the great romances of his bachelorhood'. But Tyson himself would later deny that this was so.

Nevertheless, they were often seen out together. One photographer snapped them in a restaurant, she sporting a Minnie Mouse look, all ribbons and bows. Both beam blatantly for the camera as they raise their forks to their lips. Another shot depicts a very youthful-looking Naomi administering a firm right hook to Tyson's valuable chin, as he clutches her forearm with a mock grimace.

Females were always throwing themselves at the boxer, according to Naomi. She reported how women would approach him when they were out together, not caring that he had a woman on his arm. 'They'd go up to him and grab him and kiss him in front of me. And he used to say, "That's my girlfriend sitting there!" and they'd say, "We don't care!"' Naomi told how, when she was in Las Vegas with Tyson, girls would hang around downstairs in droves, fighting each other to get up to his room, knocking on his bedroom door at all hours of the day and night.

Because of the way women behaved towards him, Tyson believed he could have anyone he wanted. Plentiful were the females who took advantage of this weakness. But none appeared so calculating as the one who persuaded him to marry her right under Naomi's nose.

Naomi was getting used to this new-found level of fame as Tyson's girlfriend. Her name attached to his was guaranteed box office. The media attention surrounding him was frenzied and bound to rub off on her, securing her acres of news space and feeding the myth of the 'woman of mystery' she so desperately wanted to become. It was all working out really nicely. But then Tyson fell into the clutches of a TV starlet who was to betray his trust so monstrously that it would prove his emotional downfall.

From the moment he met Robin Givens his life careered out of control like an articulated truck without a driver. Cool, beautiful, cultivated, aloof, and mildly famous as Darlene in ABC TV's *Head of the Class*, Givens was the kind of girl Tyson thought he could never have. He was therefore determined to have her – in spite of the fact that he was in two minds about it. The lisping Brownsville hood in him said a girl like her would never look at him twice. But the heavyweight champ, the celebrity stud, knew he could have her at the snap of a finger. The two Tysons moved in on her, and Givens was ready for both.

Friends later revealed that she and her mother had been plotting to marry her off to a black celebrity for years. Distasteful little schemes involving stars such as Eddie Murphy and athlete Michael Jordan had backfired, and Tyson showed his face at just the right time.

After an unorthodox courtship, during which Givens apparently fell pregnant, the couple were married on 7 February 1988. Their wedding came as a huge surprise to almost everyone close to Tyson, including his managers. It was a bit of a shock for Naomi, too, who had been with Tyson herself only a few days earlier. She read about it in the papers like everyone else.

The marriage brought Tyson no happiness. Givens claimed a miscarriage, and just eight months later she and her mother nailed the coffin by betraying Tyson on television as a domestic brute and a wife-beater. As her husband, doped to the eyeballs with the drugs for his so-called manic depression, sat dumbly beside her, Givens claimed that she lived in terror and that, had it not been for herself and Mommie Dearest, Tyson would definitely have 'killed himself or somebody else'.

Naomi was just one of millions who watched the television interview in utter disbelief. 'Just knowing him, I knew that wasn't true,' she said. 'I cried when I saw it. I was filming *The Cosby Show*, and we'd finished shooting, and the television came on, and everyone just kind of sat there and watched it. I remember I looked at Bill [Cosby] and just started crying. I felt very sad for Mike at that point.'

The much-heralded fight between Tyson and Frank Bruno took place at the Las Vegas Hilton on 25 February 1989, and proved another swift victory for the Brownsville Boy. Don King, the preposterous fright-haired promoter and former Cleveland crook, had become the driving force in Tyson's life, and the champion's profile was at a peak. So, too, was his personal fortune – at upwards of $200 million, the biggest pile ever amassed by a prizefighter. Also at a summit – though she would, of course, go on to scale even greater peaks – was the image of eighteen-year-old Naomi, the 'Sarf London modelle' who had honed herself into a breathtakingly beautiful, perfectly poised, sophisticated member of the international jet-set. Within hours of spotting her in Las Vegas at the ringside during the Tyson-Bruno fight, most of the world's press had the couple engaged. Naomi laughed it off, but there was more to it than met the eye.

Just weeks into this second attempt at a relationship with Tyson she began sporting a huge diamond ring, inviting speculation. But then her mother unwittingly revealed that the ring had been a present from a man that she herself had lived with. Or *was* it?

Much later, an American dancer called Trena Archie claimed in the newspapers that she had caught Naomi in bed with Tyson in Vegas when he was supposed to be *her* boyfriend. 'I was shocked,' said Archie. 'Mike had invited me to his suite for a party, but when his friends let me in they told me that he was busy. I looked into the bedroom and saw four bare legs thrashing about. It was Naomi and Mike. I was very unhappy about it.' The real reason for Archie's distress emerged later: at the time she was carrying what was apparently Tyson's child. Soon afterwards, she gave birth to a son, Jaston.

'When Mike came out, he apologised for keeping me waiting but said: "Naomi flew all the way from England to see me, I just couldn't ignore her." Later that night, continued Archie, Naomi came looking for her. 'I took a cab home after the party,' she reported. 'I'd only been at home thirty minutes when Naomi arrived at my apartment in a rage. She screamed at me: "You bitch, don't you dare make love to Mike again. He doesn't love you, he only loves me. If you ever fuck Mike again, I'll kill you." I thought for a minute she was going to attack me . . . she was drunk, and I couldn't believe this was the beautiful model who graced glossy magazine covers worldwide. I learned later that she was a very jealous person.' Naomi herself has neither denied nor admitted this story.

Whatever the ins and outs of Naomi's liaison with Mike Tyson – and there is no doubt that for a while they were intimate – it put Naomi on the map. In a newspaper interview in November 1992, even her own mother thanked the boxer for lending her his lime-light. 'It was Naomi's relationship with Mike Tyson that made her famous. Everyone wanted to know who was the London model dating Tyson. He is so sweet, so shy, that he hid behind Naomi's door when I met him for the first time in her New York apartment. He always called me "Ma'am" and treated me with the greatest re-spect.'

And Loana Morrison, lively columnist on black newspaper *The Voice*, commented: 'Naomi made her debut on the back of Mike Tyson, there is no doubt. Tyson was huge – how much bigger can you get than the heavyweight champion of the world? From there she had the name, the clothes, the knack of being photographed with the right people . . . from Tyson onwards it was only ever going to be famous boyfriends for Naomi. She doesn't pick up back-room boys, you know!'

Tyson, for his part, referred to Naomi as 'My little English prin-cess'. He even confided in those who he hoped were his friends that she would make the 'ideal wife' for him – that she had 'everything he looked for' in a woman. There is no question in the minds of those close to Naomi that for a spell, however brief, they had been lovers. One top model who begged for anonymity – 'She'll kill me if she knew I talked to you' – confided: 'It wasn't exactly what you could call a match made in heaven. Mike was obviously besotted for a while, and she seemed very keen on him. Whether she would have been if he was a cab driver instead of the heavyweight champion of the world, it's hard to say. There's definitely a side to Naomi that is addicted to glitz and glamour, and a famous boyfriend and eventually a famous husband, to her, is like a divine right. It's like it's a compulsory thing – she doesn't see why she should settle for anything less.'

A former colleague of Tunisian designer Azzedine Alaia recalls a visit to the designer's Paris studio. 'His place was stuffed with bodies – it was just before the Collections and everyone was going crazy. Naomi was there, dressed in this skimpy cotton dress and a pair of red boxing gloves. I remember her standing in front of the mirror throwing mock jabs at her own reflection. There was a photograph of Mike Tyson on the wall . . . he was referred to quite openly as "Naomi's boyfriend" – everyone knew they were an item.'

The relationship fizzled, ultimately, because of distance and lifestyle. 'They were both all over the place all the time,' said Naomi's model friend. 'Their lives were controlled by people who wanted their money's worth. One of them would have had to give up what they were doing in order to be with the other full-time, and neither of them was in a position to do that. What's more, you have to remember that they were both really young, and he was far more immature than she was. He probably never grew up as a personality.'

Feisty *Harpers and Queen* editor Vicki Woods, who interviewed them both for American *Vogue*, was amazed that they ever got it together in the first place. 'He was like a child, but menacing at the same time,' she says of the former champion whom she interviewed in his Las Vegas bedroom in 1992. 'It was impossible for me to imagine that this young black guy could actually have the hots for a logical, thinking, forty-three-year-old mother of two. The rational part of my brain was saying, "There's something wrong with this poor boy", and what was wrong was that he was coming *on* to me!

'It was all rather threatening. There was a lot of physical connection. He has giant hands. You know, he brushes the hair off your forehead and the room goes dark. His footwork was excruciating, and it's embarrassing even to think about it. I was wriggling away from him on the sofa and being really bright and Mumsie. It was like dealing with a very over-sized three-year-old. I just had to keep laughing.

'He had drawings done by children all over the walls. He had an "Aw, Shucks" little-American-kid kind of voice. He kept patting the bed he went and sat on, and said, "Come. Sit down. Let's relax. Let's hang out a little.' And he kept telling Don King he didn't want to talk about money – he wasn't interested in the money. I was terrified he might lose his temper any minute, and swat me across the room like a fly.'

Naomi, on the other hand, seemed to Woods so slick, so street-smart and so together when the two women met in New York that she couldn't imagine how Naomi and Tyson had ever found anything to say to each other. 'She looks like something that walked straight out of a dream. And she is very, very sharp and in control. She calls the shots. The day of our interview, she kept me waiting for an hour and three-quarters. Every five minutes I'd say, 'Ring her flat and tell her I'm still in the lobby.' And they'd say, "Lady, listen, we'll be surprised if she gets down here by this afternoon. This is what happens."'

Woods had seen Naomi at work before, and pronounced her 'brilliantly professional'. 'She's great when she gets on the runway. She's energetic, she gets in and out of clothes, she's assiduous, she doesn't fuss. A professional to the nth degree. Off-stage, she's a nightmare. It's as if she was born to be a New Yorker. She is a parody: the epitome of a New York Supermodel, who goes out in the morning in the Azzedine jacket, Lycra leggings and dark glasses. We jumped in a cab. The restaurant she wanted to eat at was closed, so we ended up somewhere near Bloomingdale's. She was wearing dark glasses. She didn't want this, she didn't want that. She kept saying things like 'What kind of place *is* this?' and kept waving her little hand. She was petty and sulky, she didn't want waiters, she was waving them away. She looked like she'd had too many late nights, but still lovely, and she'd lost all her eyebrows and they won't grow back. But she is *luminous* when she is being photographed . . .'

In February 1992, when an Indiana jury voted to convict Mike Tyson of the rape of eighteen-year-old Miss Black America contestant Desirée Washington of Rhode Island, even sports writers cheered the decision against the sad character who had come to be known as a 'serial buttocks-fondler'. What really happened between the two in Room 606 of the Canterbury Hotel, Indianapolis in July 1991 only two people could tell, and one of them was lying. Whatever the outcome of Tyson's appeal there are plenty who never doubted his innocence for a second, and Naomi is one of them. In October 1992, during a live British TV interview with Paula Yates for Channel 4's *The Big Breakfast*, Naomi revealed that she had written a series of affectionate letters to her former boyfriend in jail. And she said she still refused to believe that he could possibly be guilty of rape.

'I have known the man for four years and he was never that way with me, ever,' she said. 'Mike was a friend of mine and still is. I write to him, yes. I'd love to receive letters if I was in an isolated place.'

When I contacted Mike Tyson in prison through a mutual friend on American journal Sports Illustrated, he was reluctant to comment on his feelings for Naomi. 'I really don't want to say very much about her,' was his response to my questions. 'She never meant that much to me, actually.' It was a strange comment from someone who had once suggested that for him she would make the perfect wife.

They had more in common than perhaps they ever realized. Both had lifted themselves out of the ghetto and risen to the top rung on what appeared to be physical attributes and grim determination alone: he with his fists, and she with her looks. It was animal and not intellectual instincts which had fuelled their success. And

when they found themselves moving in powerful circles, it was attitude which saw them through. Both were perceived by the public to
be something other that what they are. Perhaps they recognized
this, and shared an unspoken empathy. His image had been stacked
against him as the world's most loathsome brute, all to ensure ticket
sales. Naomi's image portrayed her as the tough but classy, accom-
plished and soignée woman-of-the-world. It only looked that way.
Beauty and the Beast: there couldn't have been a more perfect
example. Another time, another place, they might have made the
perfect match.

8

Robert De Niro's Waiting . . .

A balmy evening in 1983. A drop-dead gorgeous green-eyed blonde with vanilla skin all over is drinking at the bar of the chic Jackie O. club in Rome. She lifts her champagne glass with one hand, her skein of pale yellow hair away from her head with the other. Stippled into the skin at the nape of her neck is a livid dragon tattoo. She is wearing a gold bra to match her gleaming stilettos, and her cupidic mouth pouts through its bright scarlet gloss.

'As I flipped my head and swivelled on my bar stool I noticed these two guys approaching me, and I recognized one of them immediately,' remembers Anna Moana Pozzi, the Italian porn film star and millionairess, more recently a candidate for the Love Party and successor to La Cicciolina in her country's 1992 political elections. 'He came straight up to me and said: "You look like you fuck like a black woman."

'It was Robert de Niro. It made me laugh, but I didn't like him for it. They told me they were in Italy filming *Once Upon a Time in America*. We drank all night together, and Bob was nice to me, but I didn't find him attractive. He was very scruffy, with scuffed shoes, old trousers and a sweater that had definitely seen better days. His actor friend, Harvey Keitel, was much sexier, so I went to bed with him instead.'

'YOU LOOK LIKE YOU FUCK LIKE A BLACK WOMAN.' Never was a preference more succinctly stated. De Niro's taste for dusky dames is well known to the point that he is frequently dubbed 'The Coalminer' in showbiz circles. Naomi Campbell, twenty-seven years his junior, was sadly just another maiden in a long exotic line.

If her friendship with Mike Tyson signalled the genesis of her international fame, it was her affair with Bob De Niro that sealed it. Despite his wild streak, De Niro is an intensely private star who shuns publicity and has always made plain to the media, at times aggressively, that his personal life should remain that way; that those who dared to pry would be sorry. Ever eager to improve herself, Naomi would soak up whatever she could from those whom she regarded as her 'betters'. She quickly cottoned on to the fact that absolute discretion was the key to a relationship with this one. If she kept her mouth shut, she was in with a chance. The couple dated secretly for almost two years before American gossip columnist Richard Johnson broke the exclusive in the *New York Daily News*.

'Robert De Niro is good at keeping a secret,' he wrote on 3 April 1991.

He has been having a torrid affair with cover girl Naomi Campbell for more than a year, and hardly anyone knew. 'I wouldn't say they went out together – more like they stayed *in*', is the way one source put it. They were never seen together in public. De Niro is usually photographed with his long-time main squeeze, Toukie Smith. But it's more than coincidence that De Niro and Naomi have the same lawyer, Allen Grubman. The romance would have stayed secret if Naomi were as discreet as De Niro. She isn't. The Elite model, a former ballet dancer, was so distraught after a lover's quarrel with De Niro that she had to be hospitalised.

Many more facts about their relationship would come to light after it ended than ever emerged while it endured.

As an actor, De Niro has often been described as 'predatory'. He seems possessed of a sometimes demonic and overpowering masculinity, not unlike Mike Tyson's, which frightens and compels so effectively on screen because that barely concealed rage and violence in the sort of trapped man he portrays is almost tangible. He was *The Last Tycoon* in 1976, the enigmatic Vito Corleone of *The Godfather Part II* in 1974, and the primitive Jake La Motta in *Raging Bull* of 1980, for which he won his Oscar. In his legendary preparation for the part, De Niro literally became La Motta. He was coached by the fighter himself for over a year, as well as by the trainer responsible for Sylvester Stallone as Rocky. For the latter half of the film, in which he had to portray the obese, self-destructive monster into which La Motta metamorphosed, De Niro scoffed himself across Europe to gain 60 pounds and jeopardized his health in so doing.

As Travis Bickle, the deranged urban avenger in *Taxi Driver* of 1976, and as the steel-worker in *The Deerhunter* of 1978, trying to come to terms with his unthinkable experiences in Vietnam, De Niro was immediately identifiable with the victims of the age. In 1977's *New York New York* for which he learned from scratch to play the saxophone, his domineering, chauvinist-pig character tells Liza Minnelli's: 'You don't say goodbye to me, I say goodbye to *you*.'

'I can't cheat when I act', he has said. 'I know that the cinema is an illusion, but not for me.' For all their macho posturing, De Niro's characters frequently wound up as romantic losers.

As in art, so in life. At fifty, permanent happiness with one partner still eludes him. And almost every woman in his life has been black, indicating nothing less than an obsession to those who have ever paused to analyse it. 'I have a theory about De Niro's women,' said one long-time acquaintance. 'They decorate his life with their exotic looks and egregious ways. These magnificent black women with their spontaneity and self-assurance fill him with joy and respect. He is *very* Italian in many ways. You see it in his courtly behaviour towards women.'

A former United Airlines stewardess corroborated this assessment. She told me: 'It was well known among the airline staff that Robert De Niro liked black women. If ever there was a cute black attendant working the flight, they'd always change the rota around so that the black girl would work first class, which of course he always travelled. It's said that more than a few of them went off with him at the end of a flight. It's a family, the staff at United, and this was not even "gossip", it was apparently common knowledge.'

In June 1976 he married the black actress Diahnne Abbott and adopted her eight-year-old daughter Drina. Together they had a son, Raphael – named after the Rome hotel in which he was conceived. 'What a sweet romantic name,' quipped the actress Shelley Winters. 'I'm just glad they weren't staying at the Hilton.'

Lasting happiness was not to be. It was rumoured that the couple parted because Diahnne liked the high life and De Niro didn't. But this theory did not hold water if his subsequent relationship with another black beauty, Toukie Smith, was anything to go by, since here was a girl who, like Naomi, did not exactly shun a shindig. The marital bust-up may have had more to do with media reports that De Niro had fathered, in September 1982, the child of ebony-skinned nightclub entertainer Helena Lisandrello, who also used the stage name Helena Springs. Instead of being shattered by the revelation, De Niro showered Lisandrello with presents, including clothes and a sports car, and accepted the child, who was named Nina Nadjena De Niro, as his own.

Ten years after the birth, Lisandrello unfathomably filed a paternity suit against De Niro through Marvin 'Mr Palimony' Mitchelson, who had also acted for Natalie Fears in her paternity claim against Mike Tyson. When the results of a paternity test ordered by a California court were published, it emerged that De Niro could not be the father of the child whom her mother calls Nina De Niro. Lisandrello, nonplussed, announced plans to continue with her claim for $5000 per month maintenance from De Niro on the grounds that 'he represented to the child that he was her father'.

'It's such "A Thing" here now,' Naomi told me during our interview in New York, 'women having babies and getting the men to pay, and then the men finding out later it's not their baby. All for money! I feel so bad when it happens. A relationship with someone must be based on love, not money.' It was a thinly disguised attack on Lisandrello – perhaps on De Niro's behalf. The star triumphed in the end: in April 1993 the Los Angeles Superior Court ruled that, as De Niro had been proven not to be the girl's biological father, he no longer had to continue payments.

bove: with Elton John
bove right: Iman and Herb Ritts
ight: Christy Turlington, Gianni
ersace and Cindy Crawford
elow: Sylvester Stallone

Fluffing her lines at Elite's
Plaza Hotel model show

With bosom buddy Linda
Evangelista

At the New York première for Madonna's movie *Truth or Dare*

A rare sighting at the Paris Ritz with Robert De Niro

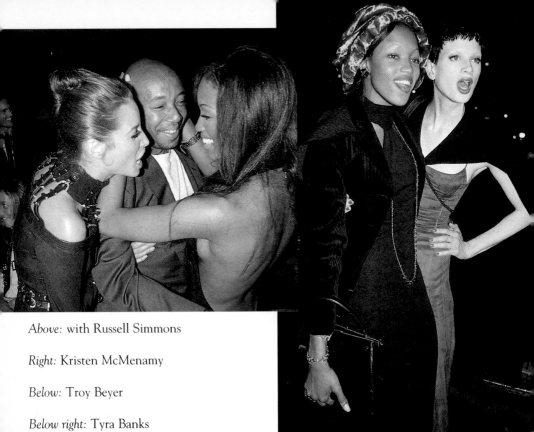

Above: with Russell Simmons

Right: Kristen McMenamy

Below: Troy Beyer

Below right: Tyra Banks

Although he has made several significant movies in recent years – *GoodFellas, Awakenings, Guilty by Suspicion, Night and the City, Cape Fear* – it must irk him that the thing about him which fascinates us most is his private life. Like Michael Jackson he is a master of disguise, moving easily about New York as well as more far-flung places in wigs, spectacles and hats, and sometimes even sheltering beneath a golf umbrella. He walks stealthily and swiftly. He is leaner, plainer, more lank-locked than you'd imagine. He is invariably scruffy, and if he has a sense of humour he doesn't care to let it show. He'll talk to you, these days, if it's films you want to know about. But veer too closely towards his personal life, or dare to ask questions about Naomi Campbell, and he'll deftly but menacingly steer the conversation back to his work, or leave the room altogether.

'I was *not* seeking a father-figure! Age has nothing to do with why I am attracted to a man,' Naomi insisted in 1992 when I quizzed her about her affair with De Niro.

Still, she had to admit, twenty-seven years is a hefty enough age gap.

'Really? Well, I don't comment on my personal life!' she trilled like a budgie, as if quoting from a script De Niro might have written himself.

Nevertheless, she could not deny that the actor was at that point her Main Squeeze.

'Well, what can I say? The papers all have pictures of us together, so I can't deny it.' Although she had been doing just that for some time.

What on earth did they have in common, the ageing actor and the kittenish clothes-horse, apart from a passion for desert islands, designer pasta, ice cream, and the occasional Big Mac and fries? Not so much, on the face of things.

'And yet she adored him,' remembers Linda Stein, New York realtor to the stars and former wife of Seymour Stein, the Sire

Records chief and pioneer of New York's New Wave punk scene in the late 1970s. Linda, who knew both De Niro and Naomi socially, was not the only one who could not recall how they had first met.

'How'd she meet him? I don't know! Famous people just meet in New York and LA, they go to each other's parties, they attend charity events, they just *meet* – *you* know how it works! All I know is that she met him frequently, and she called him "Bobby". They were sweet together. What can I tell you?'

When gossip columnist Richard Johnson first revealed their affair in the *New York Daily News* in April 1991 it emerged that the couple were not only sharing the same lawyer, New York hot-shot Allen Grubman, but it was also alleged that Naomi had already swallowed the first of her infamous 'overdoses' following a lovers' tiff, and had spent the night in hospital as a result. Whether Naomi's reported suicide attempts are true is not known, but she has not officially denied them, whatever the truth.

Such behaviour constituted the classic cry for help. And it may, perhaps, be a more definite indication of Naomi's deep-rooted insecurity and lack of true self-worth than anything else. Psychiatrists identify the failed suicide attempt – it was never *meant* to succeed – as one of the most desperate of attention-grabbing measures. It is designed to provoke guilt in the other party, to make them sit up and take notice of the 'victim', feel sorry for them, and lavish upon them the attention they crave.

'Attention-seeking measures, attempted suicides, are all about love and admiration and adoration, and how to achieve these things,' an eminent psychiatrist explained. 'Marilyn Monroe was the absolute personification of this. Also, a young girl hankering after a much older and more successful man is probably seeking a father-figure, however hard she protests against that. We may be talking about an unstable personality who has never achieved a strong sense of Self, who believes that she is only loved for her image, but is panicking deep inside: "Nobody really *knows* me. Nobody likes me for myself. I *am* just a pretty face and a nice body." It is desperately sad. She doesn't feel lovable unless someone else is loving her to an extreme level. She's a person who appears to have everything in life – but she doesn't, not really. She will never have that until she learns to love herself.'

Naomi quickly set her sights on De Niro as her ideal husband-to-be. But softly, softly would she catch this most unpredictable of monkeys, and maybe not even then. When I asked her, at the height of their affair, if she would marry her illustrious lover, she replied, coy as a choirgirl:

'He'll have to ask me first!'

He clearly had not. But had she asked *him? 'No!* I've never asked anyone! I'm rather hoping I won't have to – that someone will ask *me!'*

The British press, of course, milked the De Niro-Naomi affair for all it was worth. On 4 April 1991 the *Daily Star* followed up the news from America, pointing out that: 'De Niro had been secretly dating the beauty behind his girlfriend Toukie Smith's back. Toukie is now threatening to take him to the cleaners for part of his multi-million-dollar fortune.'

But it was not until March the following year that Toukie had her say, having maintained the discreet silence that De Niro had always insisted on and admired her for adhering to. The former model and actress admitted that she and De Niro had been lovers for more than eight years, but insisted: 'I am certainly *not* a rival. Robert and I were very happy, but I am sad to say that that part of my life is over.' Her message to Naomi, however, was a sharp one: 'You are welcome to him! I hope it all works out.'

In February 1992, Naomi bared her heart and soul in *Hello!* magazine, and therefore would soon fall victim to its 'Curse'. There is an unwritten law which states that every happy-ever-after celebrity who gushes about how happy they are/how wonderful life is to that cosily idealistic, Spanish-produced weekly will soon find themselves bereft, and desperately seeking a replacement live-in. The list is endless: the Yorks, the Jane Seymours, the Monacos, the Trumps, model Lisa Butcher and super-chef Marco Pierre-White – whose marriage lasted all of fifteen weeks! But the twenty-one-year-old Naomi knew little of the sad curse when she posed for *Hello!*'s photographer Frederic Meylan in a Los Angeles studio, and bleated to interviewer Françoise Menette that two years spent denying De Niro was quite long enough. In the magazine's over-cautious Question-Answer style, Menette leads us through the revelation thus:

Q.   Which is your best quality?
A.   I give everything when I'm in love.
Q.   And your worst?
A.   I bite my lips when I'm nervous.
Q.   Is that all?
A.   Perhaps also I'm too sensitive and strongly affected by things.
Q.   Are you in love now?
A.   Very much so.
Q.   Will you tell us who with?
A.   Robert De Niro. I'm not going to deny it any more.
Q.   What do you love most about him?
A.   His understanding. That he is a true friend and a support to me.
Q.   How do you envisage your future?
A.   In my private life, married and with children. I dream of that – and some day it will come true.

Facing the interview, the magazine ran a glorious full-length photograph of Naomi in an outrageously flamboyant wedding dress designed by Gianni Versace, which made even Trudi Styler's get-up for the Sting Has Stung nuptials look dull.

The *Daily Mail* fell upon the story within hours, devoting to it a whole page entitled I'M SO IN LOVE WITH DE NIRO MY GOODFELLA SAYS NAOMI. In May that year the same paper was proclaiming a coup, having despatched 'Honorary White Man', Hot Gossip columnist Baz Bamigboye, and their relentlessly smooth photographer Steve Back, on a mild goose chase to France. Not only did the dapper pair charm their way into the Paris Ritz where they commenced their stake-out, but they succeeded in getting pictures of Naomi and De Niro together, and even a brief interview with the model in the hotel's famed Hemingway Bar. When Naomi emerged from the Ritz's Place Vendôme entrance dressed in floaty frock, Chanel jacket, baseball cap, sunglasses and huge heart-shaped Chanel pendant, she was obviously pleased to see the pair and slapped on a happy face. It was a far cry from the fake-moustache disguise she had donned to sneak up to the fifth-floor suite she was sharing with De Niro when she first arrived.

Over a drink in the Hemingway Bar, she and Baz '. . . talked of life, love and her superstar sweetheart'. 'He is such a great actor and I admire him tremendously. Along with Marlon Brando he's about the best in the world, isn't he? I think he's a man who is passionate about what he does, and that makes him such a great actor. But a private life is a private life, and it's difficult to talk about the man that you love in public. My relationship should remain private because love is the most important thing to have in life, and you fight so hard for it to work that you can damage it all by talking about it.'

What was it about De Niro that excited her?

'I honestly can't tell you,' she sighed, 'but believe me, life is never dull.'

'As we talked, she toyed with a heart-shaped pendant and a sapphire ring,' reported Bamigboye. When he asked her who gave it to her, she replied: 'Just put that I bought it for myself – and that will save a whole lot of trouble.'

Her mother later told the *Daily Mirror* about the time De Niro had landed in London with a request from Naomi to call her mother. 'I'm such a fan of his!' said Valerie. 'So you can imagine how I felt when he asked me round to the Savoy Hotel. I thought he was bound to be surrounded by aides and bodyguards – I'll pop my head around the door, then disappear! But he was all by himself. And so ordinary that I couldn't believe he was this great star. He took me out to dinner . . . told me how he liked to walk around London on his own. How he'd pop into a sandwich bar because it was so important for an actor to mingle with real people and observe their behaviour. He and Naomi are still friends.'

The couple went quiet for the summer, apart from reports of Naomi's alleged street-fight with ex-*Dynasty* actress Troy Beyer, which supposedly prompted De Niro to cool it with his mercurial young girlfriend. This was denied, and the inclination is to believe him. However, De Niro's aversion to excess publicity is well known. Los Angeles-based photographer Laura Luongo recalls an incident some eight years ago in New York in which a menacing encounter with De Niro left her fearing for her life.

'I was a stringer [freelance photographer] for the *New York Post*,' Luongo explains. 'They called me up and said that Bob De Niro was seeing this play at a Broadway theatre with a woman, and could I go and get a picture of them. So I saw him walking with this woman, and I started taking pictures. He walked up and grapped me, put his arm around my neck and said: "I really don't want to hurt you – I don't like what you just did, and I want your film."'

'I was totally terrified. Did I give him the film? I *had* to! He had his hand on my neck! And, typical New York, people were just walking by us like nothing was happening. I was completely traumatized. I just put my cameras down and went back to waiting tables for a few years. Now I realize I could probably have sued the guy for mental trauma or something.'

It was during her live TV interview in London in October 1992 with Paula Yates on Channel 4's *The Big Breakfast* that Naomi revealed the affair was finally over. She admitted: 'I *like* older men. But I am not happy in love right now. I am young, free and single.' And in a pointed remark possibly aimed at De Niro, Naomi continued: 'I like honest men. I can't stand to be told something just to be told it, and it's not the truth.'

On hearing this, one colleague quipped: 'So Bobby's been up to his old tricks again. Fidelity is not exactly his forte, and Naomi is a one-man woman.' So the evidence leads us to believe. Meanwhile, in November 1992, gossip hack Sean Smith in *The People* had the pair back together again:

> The couple spent Hallowe'en dining cosily at popular Italian restaurant Barocco in Greenwich Village. They went out of their way not to attract attention, and chose a very un-celebrity table next to the kitchen. Naomi swapped her model clothes for sweatshirt and jeans . . . I am told she was very upset when she split up with De Niro . . . and she would jump at the chance of getting back together with him on a steady basis. The problem is that De Niro . . . has become more of a wolf than Jack Nicholson and Warren Beatty put together. His well-known preference is for black women . . . and he is very persistent in his pursuit of any woman.

Nobody owns Bob De Niro, though perhaps Naomi thought she could. In the end, they simply wanted different things. Naomi craved a ring on her third-left that she had not had to buy herself. She wanted a house and a garden and a couple of kids playing in the yard. She wanted someone she could call her own, whom she would not be obliged to share. But De Niro had been there, seen it, done that, eaten the cast *and* the extras. He had grown-up kids to prove it. No, his needs were simpler. His relationship with Naomi was probably not what he would classify as an affair of the heart. From where he was standing, I would imagine there were much more basic instincts involved.

The get-out clause, when it came, was a gift to tabloid journalists not too concerned with hard-and-fast facts. It had for some time been common knowledge that Naomi was being coached, by renowned New York speech therapist Sam Chwat, in an American accent. More recently, she had been learning the particular Noo Yawk bark that might secure her the female lead in a forthcoming De Niro film.

'We saw each other for about two years,' confirmed Chwat in May 1993. 'At first she was learning a basic American accent for wide applicability, to improve her career. But later, the principal impetus was that she was trying to get a role in De Niro's new movie, the one he recently wrapped, called *A Bronx Tale*. It's his directorial debut. It is based on a well-known play which received very good notices on the West Coast and in New York, to which he bought the rights. It deals with the coming-of-age of an inter-racial romance. A young Italian boy in the Bronx falls in love with a black girl, and they have a troubled affair. *Romeo and Juliet? West Side Story?* More like the De Niro-Campbell Story!

'De Niro plays the young guy's bus driver father. And you know how he applies himself. He had to get a bus driver's licence for it, so he could actually drive a bus through New York City!

'Everyone in it needed a hard New York accent. Naomi came to me to try to learn it. She studied that accent with me to the best of her ability, but finally she didn't get the part.' It went to unknown actress Taral Hicks instead.

'Naomi did learn the accent quite effectively,' he insists, 'but to be honest, I think their relationship got in the way of her getting the job.

'De Niro is the producer, of course – but for some reason, later on, he decided not to get involved in the casting,' confirms Chwat, who voice-coached De Niro for *Cape Fear* and also taught him the Seattle accent he used to such great effect in *This Boy's Life*.

'Was it difficult for me, coaching them both? Not at all. I resisted getting involved in their relationship. Let's say there were requests for judgement by him about how well she was doing, and from her side it was "Couldn't you just put in a good word for me?" – stuff like that.

'I was sorry that Naomi missed out. This might have been a big break for her. She studied with extreme diligence three or four times a week, frequently on the phone and even transatlantically when she was travelling – which she always is.'

So soon after her failure to win the role in *A Bronx Tale* did Naomi and De Niro part permanently that gossip writers refused to believe it could possibly be coincidental. As one New York journalist opined, 'I couldn't help but make a connection: the *second* Robert De Niro nixed [American slang for 'didn't'] casting Naomi Campbell in his upcoming *A Bronx Tale*, she broke the intercontinental speed record for flying to Dublin and accepted an engagement ring from U2's Adam Clayton . . .'

De Niro's publicist Stan Rosenfeld issued a statement on the matter: 'Just to set the record straight, my decision not to use Naomi in *A Bronx Tale* was based purely on a professional decision, and had no bearing on our past relationship,' read De Niro's quote. 'I've always supported her as an actress because I thought she had a very special quality. To say anything otherwise is absolute nonsense. I only wish her the best in her career and in her upcoming marriage.'

Certainly there appeared to be no hard feelings on Naomi's part. On Tuesday, 27 April 1993 an epic tribute to the career of soul queen Aretha Franklin, entitled *Duets*, was staged at the Nederlander Theater on Broadway and recorded for a Fox TV Special. It was one of those stellar nights, with everyone and his mother perfumed and present, up on stage and clapping along. Aretha sang her big heart out on the arm of Rod Stewart, Elton John, Smokey Robinson, Bonnie Raitt and all her other favourites, as non-singing celebs such as De Niro and Dustin Hoffman beamed blithely on. Spotting her former beau, a pouty smile danced across Naomi's lips as she walked right up to De Niro and planted a smacker of a kiss on his cheek . . .

'Sly! You should get over here right away and meet Naomi!' babbled real estate queen Linda Stein to her friend Sylvester Stallone at the Beverly Hills Hotel as they milled among their fellow Beautiful People. Thus began a curious relationship which was only made excruciatingly public after the event. It was all over bar the taping, it would seem.

'We were at the Beverly Hills Hotel in Los Angeles, three years ago, for this Versace Aids Benefit. It was a big week out there, lots of different events, and we all attended a *Vanity Fair* party,' recalls Stein. 'Sly is a real good friend of mine – he lived close by – and I introduced him to the Versaces and then to Naomi. That is how they met.'

They would meet, thereafter, whenever Naomi found herself working on the West Coast. And the media never even noticed. 'Naomi comes to Los Angeles about once a month, and as soon as she hits town the phone at Sly's place is ringing off the hook,' confided a friend. 'Naomi begs him to take her out, but he refuses. All their meetings are behind closed doors. She now thinks he's in it just for sex – although she's totally in love with him.'

Once again she had plumped for an older man, Stallone being twenty-four years her senior. Their alleged affair only came to light when cassettes which had preserved conversations held on Stallone's private telephone lines were leaked to the press in 1993 by a former member of his security staff. Very secure indeed. One tape appears to feature Naomi clearly pestering the star and threatening the 'overdose stunt' again unless she got to speak to him.

'I'll take a whole fucking bottle of Valium,' she warned, unaware of the eavesdropping tele-recorder. When the security guard pleaded with her not to, she retorted: 'Oh, don't worry. I've done it before, and they always catch me in time.'

When the couple *do* speak, Stallone is heard making graphic references to their apparent sex life – 'You give the best fuckin' head in the world!' – and suggesting that they have indulged together in three-way sex – the widely-held assumption is that the third person was Stallone's most recent regular girlfriend, Pretty Polly tights model Jennifer Flavin, who is affectionately known in the trade as 'Flavin of the Month'. 'Oh Sly, you're so bad!' giggles Naomi on the tape. A writ issued by Stallone's lawyers against *New York Post* columnist Richard Johnson, who quoted passages from a transcript of the tape, stated that the tapes had been illegally made and procured. Thus, with one carelessly couched piece of correspondence did Stallone damn himself and Naomi irrevocably by confirming that the tapes were authentic! In Britain the *Sun* took up the story and published extracts in its own version of the story: no writ ensued!

Though Stallone and Naomi have not commented publicly on their curious relationship, neither have they denied it. But if Robert De Niro *was* two-timing Naomi throughout their affair, then it seems she might have been getting her own back.

Had Sylvester Stallone been born in South London, or Naomi in New York City's notorious Hell's Kitchen, chances are that life would have thrown them together long before now. As familiar to her as any of the harder figures from Naomi's childhood, Stallone, like Tyson, started out on the bottom rung. He was raised by a dominant and ambitious mother. And he literally lifted himself out of obscurity with his fists.

He did study acting at the University of Miami, but his slurred speech and unusual face, the result of a careless forceps delivery, did not help. Still he trained in earnest, sometimes sleeping rough when money was tight. Then one night, just as Ali had inspired Mike Tyson to become a boxer, Stallone saw something which was to inspire the legend with which he would become indelibly linked.

On 24 March 1975, Sly watched Muhammad Ali defend the heavyweight championship against Chuck Wepner at the Coliseum in Cleveland, Ohio. Wepner, known as the Bayonne Bleeder because he always managed to get himself cut, fought bravely and was able to survive until the fifteenth round without seriously troubling Ali. But the idea of a crude no-hoper holding his own in the ring gave birth to the character of Rocky. Stallone clung like a limpet to the screenplay he subsequently wrote, insisting that only he could play the lead. For half a year he trained himself to a devastating level of fitness with former fighter Jimmy Gambina, quit carbohydrates, and swallowed a hundred vitamin capsules every day. *Rocky* was a masterpiece, and Stallone won an Oscar for the screenplay. Though he went on to make plenty of box-office hits as well as create his second alter ego, John Rambo, it was the Italian Stallion who would continue to dominate his psyche.

Stallone's love life was always turbulent. His first marriage, to the ever-faithful and supportive Sasha, had provided two sons, Sage and Seargeoh (the latter tragically diagnosed as autistic). But she later filed for divorce, claiming 'irreconcilable differences' – meaning his infidelity. His second marriage, to Great Dane Brigitte Neilsen, a mind-numbingly ambitious former model, was doomed from the start. But she did manage to use him as a springboard for her acting career – he granted her the second female lead in *Rocky IV*.

Stallone has perhaps never been completely happy in love, but at least he appears to have achieved a reasonably tranquil lifestyle. Delicious treats are part of the deal. Which star of his status would say 'No thanks' to willing playmates like Rod Stewart's ex-wife Alana, gameshow dolly Vanna White, heiress Cornelia Guest . . . or Supermodel Naomi Campbell?

It's Only Rock and Roll But I Like It!

It was perhaps inevitable that Naomi would eventually get around to the kind of men whom models are *really* interested in: the rock and rollers. After all, 'Supermodel' and 'Millionaire Rock Star' are perhaps the sexiest media titles ever coined. Alone, each stands as a synonym of wealth and glamour, evoking images of Concorde, Cristal, caviar, five-star Caribbean holidays and backstage bacchanalia. Bring them together and they make the most arresting combination of all. By comparison Politician and Call Girl, Vicar and Tart, Footballer and Page Three Pin-up all pale into inconsequence. The Supermodel is not dependent upon her man for status, style nor spending money; she is his media and material equal; she is as desirable as he is, and not just another adoring groupie – maybe for these reasons she represents the ultimate challenge. This is not to say that the equation is weighted in her favour: everybody *knows* a rock star is the biggest turn-on there is.

The model-rocker combination is not a new idea. The list rolls on and on, often referred to as the Beauty and the Beast Syndrome because gorgeousness in a rock star is not a prerequisite. The scraggier the better, in fact – it looks as if he has really lived the life.

Models, anyway, are so obsessed with their own beauty that they could hardly care less about their man's reflection. Some would say that it's because they couldn't stand the competition. But others believe that, having made an entire career out of beauty, models know better than anyone that it really *is* only skin-deep. Forget a man's surface area, it's the content that counts – substance, personality, meaningful things like that. Besides, who wants what they already have?

Super-Rock-Star and Supermodel were made for each other. It makes sense for a mannequin to date a man who understands the trappings of fame – and nobody understands it better than a rock and roller. An endless list proves the point. Bryan Ferry was dumped by Jerry Hall for Mick Jagger. Patti Boyd left George Harrison for Eric Clapton. Christie Brinkley opted for Billy Joel. Rachel Hunter claimed Rod Stewart's 'last banana in the fruit bowl' – his words. Somalian beauty Iman hooked David Bowie. And Pattie Hansen tamed Keith Richards. More modern examples include Yasmin and Simon le Bon; Estee Lauder's favourite Face, Pauline Porizkova, is hitched to the undernourished Ric Ocasek of faded rock group The Cars; Stephanie Seymour to Guns n' Roses singer Axl Rose; and sizzling Dane Helena Christiansen couldn't be more thrilled with INXS's Michael Hutchence. The Rock Around the Frock brigade had hoped for the ultimate pairing in Naomi Campbell and Adam Clayton of U2. Only time will tell. But Naomi played true to form by dipping her toe in the water with one of the big boys first . . .

'Wants to break into the rock business' is a line frequently attached to Naomi's picture in newspaper articles. And there's the rub. If you think it's an accident that Naomi manages to be seen out and about with a guitar hero just as she is trying to launch a singing career herself, you are deluded.

One highly respected executive at Michael Jackson's record company Sony, who was involved in the signing of a lucrative recording contract for Naomi (variously reported as being worth between US$1 million and US$3 million), said: 'People think there is something rather distasteful about the way a middle-aged star appears to have used this beautiful young girl. Forget it! She is much smarter than anyone realizes. She's using them! She is wild and unusual and talented, and people really underestimate her. She works her ass off. I've never known anyone work like her. Everything she does is a major commitment for her, and she puts the lot into it. She's like a fox, she has a real cunning instinct. She is also very fragile, she knows what hurts, and she doesn't get involved in anything she doesn't want to do. Don't think it's an accident that she's seen with Clapton just when she is starting to think about making records.'

'Eric Clapton? Yet another case of age before beauty,' giggled a used-to-be-young model who had the guitarist several years ago. 'Men like Eric aren't romance . . . they're *exercise* . . .'

Whether Naomi made it into Eric Clapton's bed is not actually on record – neither has commented on the rumours and neither of them is ever likely to reveal all. Given that each has enjoyed a colourful romantic past, it is not an unreasonble assumption to make. Besides, Eric's endless list of girlfriends reads like a stilettoed Hall of Fame. It seemed almost inevitable that at some point or another Naomi would get around to being linked with him. If she did, as has been suggested, contrive to be seen out with him in order to enhance her profile as the rock singer she is dying to become, the last thing she would have done would be to let him know that – she is far too smart. Clapton, on the other hand, would never have believed it in a million years anyway. Of *course* she wanted him for himself! Everyone else does. A musical genius he may be, a supremely gifted guitarist if not *the* axe hero of all time. But perhaps his greatest asset, from a girl's point of view, is that it does no harm at all to be seen out with him.

In May 1970, when Naomi Campbell was born, Clapton was already enjoying huge success as Derek of the Dominoes. He was twenty-five years old. It was with Cream that he made his name and first tasted fully blown rock star status. But drug addiction took him off the music scene for several years, and almost killed him. He wooed top sixties' model Patti Boyd away from Beatle George after 'a dawn duel' with Harrison – it was for Patti that he had written the rock classic 'Layla', and he had been determined that she would one day be his bride. But the marriage was childless, and ended after his Italian mistress Lori del Santo gave birth to his son Connor, who tragically died in a fall from a New York skyscraper when he was four years old.

Clapton is a true rock veteran, a craftsman and a survivor. His concerts are epic, emotional occasions, and hard-core blues have remained the love of his life. Naomi could learn a lot from a musician like Eric Clapton. That is not to say that he could not learn a good deal from her – particularly when it comes to fielding the media, which has never been his best subject.

It was Sean Smith of *The People* who picked up on tales from the American tabloids claiming that Eric and Naomi had been dating. On 11 October 1992 he reported:

> RED-HOT ERIC'S PLAYING IT COOL WITH CAMPBELL . . . The couple have been determined to stay out of the limelight while they get to know each other . . . both know the perils of getting carried away too quickly. The immaculately-suited Eric has always enjoyed the reputation of ladykiller. One model, who I won't name, confided he was the best lover she'd ever had . . .

In January 1993 they were seen together at the annual Rock 'n' Roll Hall of Fame awards in Los Angeles. 'They turned up together, and looked very close and they left by the back door,' reported one guest. 'But what isn't known is that they went for dinner the following night at Bill Bouquet's restaurant, just the two of them, and you'd have to be more than good friends to take a girl there.'

Naomi had been shrugging off the rumours for months. Back in October 1992 she had told a *Daily Express* reporter while out on a shopping spree in London's Camden Market: 'I know Eric Clapton, but I'm not having a secret affair with him. I love his music and I think he's a great artist, but the other stuff I don't know. It's news to me. He's a very nice person, very humble . . . I went to his concert in New York, and I went backstage and said "Hi!", but I didn't see him in Milan.'

She certainly stepped out with him in LA. The evidence, a cosy-snuggly photograph of the two of them, was there for all the world to see.

There is a great difference, or there should be, between all the men a girl gads about with when she is young, expensive and single and the man she eventually marries. Curiously, her whirlwind romance with Adam Clayton was the one relationship Naomi never attempted to hide from the press. Not that she had been ashamed of the others – far from it. But this time, it seemed, she knew it was for real, and that her man wanted it as much as she did. She seemed serenely sure about what she was doing. Could it be that Naomi's dissatisfaction with her previous boyfriends made her all the more tenacious with this one, determined as she was to hang on to a good thing? That they entered into such a swift betrothal might be deemed alarming in some circles. It came as no surprise, on 19 August 1993, when Naomi and Adam admitted in the newspapers that they had 'postponed' their wedding, possibly until next year, due to pressures of work. 'Insiders' immediately began to speculate that the verdict on the wedding was more likely to be 'possibly never'. Will it ever take place? Only time, and Adam and Naomi themselves, will tell.

Unless you are a lifelong U2 addict or at least a discerning rock fan, chances are you had never even heard of Adam Clayton until his name went up in headlines alongside Naomi's. Think U2 and you can probably picture their lead singer Bono – the long-haired, handsome, earnest one. But the rest of the band, to most people, are a bit of a blur. Think U2 and you can still see Bono, eight years on, leaping down into the throng from a scorched Wembley stage – his 'leap of faith' – plucking a young girl from the crowd and dancing a tender waltz with her that literally moved the world to tears.

13 July 1985. They danced and they sang, that day, to feed the world. It sounds a little far-fetched now, but it was probably the most honest day in the history of rock and roll. 'Even journalists cried,' quipped Live Aid's blessed, foul-mouthed mastermind Bob Geldof. 'Thousands cried. *Millions* cried.'

On a good night, U2 had shown themselves to be capable of generating an almost Who-like presence, enthusiastically endorsed by the New Jersey Messiah himself, Bruce Springsteen. That day they surpassed themselves, and it became obvious to many of us that U2 would soon emerge as the Who's natural successors. For the band who had formed in Ireland in 1979 and had for six years enjoyed a committed following, the Live Aid exposure projected them as if overnight from politically-and-socially-aware preachy cult band into mainstream international superstars. It was the last reason why they had agreed to take part – and nobody could have been more surprised than U2 themselves that the whole world suddenly seemed to want a piece of them. Their performance at Live Aid was without doubt the most thrilling, the most memorable, the most moving. Today, they have sold an estimated 50 million copies of albums such as *The Unforgettable Fire*, *The Joshua Tree*, *Rattle and Hum*, and *Achtung Baby*. Thanks largely to the sale of their label Island Records in 1989, each member of the band is a multi-millionaire in his own right. But U2 are widely regarded as the world's greatest as well as the richest rock supergroup. Their music, like the Beatles', has universal appeal.

Perhaps the most appealing thing about U2 is that they appear to be unchanged by their mega-success. They are still the boys-next-door. They still live in Ireland, albeit in palatial dwellings these days, but at least they didn't turn their backs on home and head for New York or California, which is what rock stars usually do – at least for a while.

'Everyone in the world looks up to success,' remarked Bono once. 'But in Dublin they actively despise it. That's why we stay there.' Their achievements have not gone unnoticed. The local tax office has had to open an entire department just to deal with the band members' revenue. And since the signing of their latest contract in June 1993 – £130 million for their next six albums – the band and their manager are now five of the richest men in Ireland, the U2 industry being one of that economy's most important assets. Indeed, in the history of pop only Michael Jackson has signed a more lucrative contract. U2 now earn more than some multinational companies. Their 1992 US tour grossed £68 million, and 1993's 'Zooropa' tour should do the same again.

The fact that three of them – Paul 'Bono Vox' Hewson, drummer Larry Mullen Jnr and guitar-and-keyboard player Dave 'The Edge' Evans – are committed Christians may say much about why they have managed to stay on the straight and narrow when by this time most other rock and rollers of their stature and resources have strayed. Adam Clayton, however, is what you might call the Black Sheep. There is always one.

He was born on 13 March 1960 in Chinnor, Oxfordshire. His father, Brian, was a pilot in the Royal Air Force, and his mother, Jo, had been an air stewardess. When Adam was five years old his father joined Aer Lingus and the family moved to Malahide, a comfortable middle-class town about eight miles outside Dublin.

With his sister Sarah Jane, known as Sindy, and his brother Sebastian, who was born in Dublin, he enjoyed a normal, fairly uneventful childhood. He attended Castle Park, a typical preparatory school in Dalkey, across Dublin, and at thirteen transferred to St Columba's College, a co-ed boarding school in Rathfarnham at the foot of the Dublin Mountains.

Though clearly very bright, Adam was indifferent to his lessons, and his rebellious nature began to get the better of him. The more his teachers tried to discipline him, the more difficult he became. When his got his first bass guitar – for which his parents paid the then princely sum of £57 – he lost interest in everything but music. He was sometimes to be seen streaking through the school corridors at odd hours. And the hippy clothes, caftans, Arab head-dresses and dark glasses he took to wearing to school were deemed unacceptable, so that eventually he was forced to leave. In September 1976 he was moved to Mount Temple free school, Ireland's first 'progressive comprehensive', where he would remain for two years. It was here that he met Paul Hewson, Larry Mullen and Dave Evans, who were soon to become his partners in crime.

Larry Mullen, a Catholic James Dean lookalike with a drum kit, had pinned up a card on the school notice board advertising for anyone interested in forming a band. The other three quickly signed up. With diverse backgrounds, views and interests, the only thing they appeared to have in common was that all were members of the school choir.

'Adam stuck out like a sore thumb,' said Mullen. 'He used to drink coffee in class and wore a kilt.'

At first they called themselves Feedback – a comic reference to the noise emitting from Adam's amplifier. He was said to be the least musically able of the group, but bluffed his way along with his equipment and hip industry chat. 'He had the only amplifier so we never argued with him,' recalled Mullen. 'We thought this guy must be a musician because he knew what he was talking about. He used words like "fret" and "gig" – and then we discovered he couldn't play at all.'

Then they were The Hype, and finally U2, a name for which a variety of meanings have been offered up, but which is generally taken as an invitation to everyone to take part in their music: you too can join in.

When Adam was invited to leave school he assumed the role of band manager – until they found former commercial director Paul McGuinness, who remains their manager to this day. They signed a deal with baked bean heir Chris Blackwell's Island Records, who had nurtured the careers of Bob Marley, Free, Bad Company, Steve Winwood, Cat Stevens and Grace Jones, and set about the serious business of making hit records. Suddenly, in an era of MTV and micro-chips and emulator keyboards which could pretend to be any instrument you liked, here was a raw young band with the basic guitar, bass and drum kit, committed to the hitherto unfashionable notion of reminding people what used to make rock tick.

'We were inspired by New Yorkers like Patti Smith and Television, rather than the Sex Pistols. But we did have this spark, because the music takes second place to the emotion, and that's how it is today,' said Bono.

The fact that Adam was the only non-believer in the band set him apart from the rest. Stories of him being forced to wait until the others had gone to sleep before getting wrecked with the crew are legendary. On the road, the others would huddle at the back of the tour bus reading the Bible and singing Gospel choruses. At one point it even looked as if their religious fanaticism would hijack the band and be their downfall, especially when they became briefly involved with the sinister Shalom cult. But somehow they managed to find their perspective. Adam, meanwhile, got on with being a rock star. He was certainly wild, but not dangerously so. After a show, while the others were saying their prayers and tucking each other up in bed, he'd go on the rampage – clubs, booze, girls, a pint and a rap with the locals.

'His tastes in après-concert diversion were more traditional than that of his U2 colleagues,' recalled biographer Eamon Dunphy in *The Unforgettable Fire, the Story of U2*. 'Adam and Paul [McGuinness] were close, and would look for bars and clubs, and have a few drinks after the show. Adam likes girls and had a ball. He usually slept late the next day, sometimes waking up in his own bed.'

The others were not disapproving – they merely turned a blind eye. Adam wasn't just useful with a bass guitar. Off-stage, he was the life and soul of the band. He had the gift of the gab when it came to dealing with record company types, business managers, the road crew, and marketing and publicity people. He was funny, sharp, diplomatic, well-mannered and self-deprecating. He had a nice-and-easy attitude to the whole business of being a star. He was the consummate professional when he needed to be. Otherwise he was going to get drunk, get laid and have a good time.

As the honorary Black Sheep, a couple of skirmishes with the law were almost mandatory. Adam did not disappoint. On 10 January 1985 he knocked down a motorcycle policeman and dragged him – some reports said for fifteen yards, others claimed for forty minutes! – behind his car. According to the *Irish Evening Press* he told the officer of the Garda Siochana, the Irish police, to 'stop messing around and fuck off'. He was found guilty of drink and dangerous driving, fined £225 and banned from driving for three years, which was later reduced to two after the officer told the court that Clayton had apologised.

'I was an asshole,' he later commented. 'I was drunk. But it was pretty embarrassing to see it spread all over the papers.'

In October 1989 he was further banned for a year and fined £500 for failing to produce insurance papers after driving home from a friend's engagement party while twice over the legal alcohol limit. It was his second brush with the law that year. On 6 August he had been charged with possession of 19 grammes of cannabis with intent to supply the drug to others. During his trial the judge, Justice Windle, enquired: 'How many cigarettes could you make from 19 grammes?'

'About 150,' replied the arresting officer, Garda Moody.

Windle, remarking with a chuckle that people are allowed to bring 200 cigarettes through Customs free of duty, dismissed the charge without conviction provided Adam promised to donate £25,000 to the Women's Aid Refuge Centre. Thus his record remained clear of a drug offence, and it would be business as usual for the band. Had he been charged, a criminal record might have resulted in visa applications for countries such as the United States, Japan and Australia being refused. Unable to tour in such territories, the band would almost certainly have disintegrated. After the trial, eccentric U2 fan Paul Mathews let loose twenty-five thousand cabbage white butterflies in a park outside Dublin – one for every pound his idol had shelled out for the fine.

A bespectacled, oft-unshaven bleached blond with pallid and sometimes spotty skin – thanks to a lifestyle which could hardly be described as organic, and invariably dressed in a black leather jacket and grubby jeans, Adam was never what you'd call a classic heartthrob. He looks more like an impoverished undergraduate than the Millionaire Rock Star. But, as the only seriously unattached member of the band, he was one of rock's most eligible bachelors. Bono has been happily married to Ali for more than ten years and the couple have two daughters. Larry Mullen has had the same girlfriend, Anne Achieson, for over seven years. And while The Edge's marriage to Aislinn – the couple have three children – broke up under the strain of the U2 lifestyle, they have been trying to pick up the pieces.

Thus Adam never found himself wanting for female company. He was once, in 1986, linked to Clannad singer Maire Ni Bhraonain, but steady girlfriends were not usually on the agenda. Blondes, brunettes and redheads, they launched themselves at Clayton in their droves, and who was he to say no? But whatever he got up to, he was always impeccably tight-lipped. He had joked once or twice that the only thing missing from his life was Naomi Campbell. Adam had admired the Supermodel from afar for years, but their gold-paved paths had never crossed. When finally they did, early in 1993, it was time for some serious love at first sight. The press had a field day. No two headlines agreed. But if the facts didn't tally, the result was still sensational.

Adam's obsession with Naomi really took hold when he saw his heart's desire wrapped around Madonna across the pages of porn volume *Sex*, and wouldn't stop harping on about it. He was, in fact, no stranger to nudity himself: late in 1991 he had posed full-frontal for a photograph to be used on the cover of U2's latest album, *Achtung Baby*. But when it emerged that the picture might cause the record to be banned in America and Japan, it was almost dropped.

The shot was finally incorporated in a multi-frame montage, and fell on the back of the cover. So small and blurred was the red-silhouetted result that one couldn't actually see what it was. The following February, at the Irish Music Awards Ceremony, Bono stunned guests when he walked out on stage and declared: 'Adam Clayton has the smallest willie in the band.' Clayton wasn't too put out . . . after all, *he* was the only one who has been brave enough to pose in the nude.

It was only a matter of time before fate could be coerced into lending a hand in Adam's ideal love affair. Incredibly, following a series of coincidences, Naomi found herself, less than three months after their first meeting, listening transatlantically to those four little words she had always longed to hear.

It had all begun when Michael Jackson's producer, Quincy Jones, sent her a cutting of an interview with Adam in which he was asked what in the world he didn't already have that he really wanted, and he answered: 'A date with Naomi Campbell.' She was flattered, but thought nothing of it until she and her buddies, photographer Steven Meisel and Benjamin Forrest, attended a U2 concert in New York. Backstage, she met Adam and the rest of the band briefly, and that was that. But a few days later, now in Europe as is her wont, she missed a Concorde flight back to New York. Also on the next available plane was Bono, with whom she sat and chatted. And the chat naturally got around to Adam's crush on Naomi. Bono also invited her to a farewell party for long-time Principal Management executive Ellen Darst in New York, who had represented the band for years.

In February, Naomi was asked to hand out one of the prizes at the Brits Music Awards in London, where U2 won best Live Act. At the post-presentation party, she once again found herself chatting with Bono and Adam Clayton. Back in New York now, Naomi missed another flight, this time to Los Angeles where she was to attend the Grammy Awards, the Music Industry's Oscars. Reseated on another plane, she happened to find herself travelling with Clayton, who had himself stopped off in New York on his way to the Grammys. Thence began a flying romance which leaves you breathless just to think about it.

On 17 March 1993, during Paris Fashion Week, Naomi took a now famous catwalk tumble from a pair of ludicrous Vivienne Westwood platform shoes which resulted in cute but embarrassing knicker shots being splashed across tabloid front pages all over the world. A reel of the mishap was even shown that night on *News At Ten*. But, unbeknown to the press at that point, she was involved in a much juicier little scheme that week which probably closed the deal for Clayton.

Egged on by Bono's wife Ali, Naomi had agreed to take part in a live satellite link-up between Dreamchaser, the company which produces U2's videos, in association with a willing French TV company, and Adam Clayton's Rathfarnham, Dublin home. From Paris, Naomi, Yasmin le Bon and two other models sang 'Happy Birthday' live to Adam for his thirty-third. At the end of the song, they pulled open their tops to reveal the words 'Happy Birthday Adam' written in lipstick across their expensive chests. A 'tired and emotional' Simon le Bon apparently joined in the tribute towards the end.

After that, the love affair took off at a rate of knots. On Thursday, 18 March she arrived at Adam's home for a brief holiday. On Monday the 22nd they made their first appearance together in public, at a Duran Duran concert in Dublin's National Stadium. Naomi looked low-key chic in a black velvet jacket slit at the sides, and black leggings. After the show they met up with Simon and Yasmin le Bon backstage before driving off in Adam's white Volkswagen Golf. The couple were seen out and about over the next few days, walking hand in hand through Dublin's fair city and canoodling at various restaurants and nightclubs, such as the brunch haunt Baton Rouge on St Stephen's Green, and Lillie's Bordello nightclub, which hosted Bono's party for his wife Ali's birthday.

Every move they now made, every breath they exhaled, the press were on to them. Naomi, the whole of Dublin knew the morning after, made a point of visiting Firenze, stockists of highly covetable Irish Lainey Keogi sweaters, where she bought – shock! horror! – a cornflower-blue knit dress for about £389. The couple were even spotted in Marks and Spencer's Food Hall. *Was* that a can of baked beans they were buying? Is there no *end* to the excitement? Reporters were in their element – a pork pie in a phone box for a business lunch is bearable when the doorstepping is as easy as this! Naomi also spent a good deal of time hanging around The Factory rehearsal studios where U2 had begun to prepare for their European tour.

On Friday, 30 April she again left New York for Dublin, arriving that evening; the following night she appeared live on a popular Irish TV chat show and announced her engagement. She was driven to the RTE Network studios in a Mercedes, accompanied by Clayton and two female friends who sat among the studio audience. She was wearing a long, white, kimono-style coat-dress patterned with a 'patchwork quilt' design, a black ribbon choker and ropes of black beads wound around both wrists. Her hair was cropped boyishly short to reveal her beautiful, radiant face. She looked blissfully happy when she came on to be interviewed by Pat Kenny, host of the *Kenny Live* show.

During the interview she was routinely asked if she would ever consider marrying an Irishman. She did not hesitate over her reply, and delivered it with glee: 'I *am* marrying an Irishman!' she giggled, her face lighting up like Las Vegas on Christmas Eve as she flashed a dazzling diamond and emerald ring. 'I got it last night when I flew in from New York,' she revealed.

Kenny could have kissed her for granting him this exclusive. She told him that she and Adam had been introduced by singer Bono after a U2 concert in New York.

'It was just, "Hello, how are you?" Then I met him again at a party I went to in New York, and we started talking.' Soon afterwards in February, she confirmed, she missed her flight to Los Angeles for the Grammy Awards, and she and Adam wound up on the same flight. 'We sat together,' she said. 'I think it was love at first sight' – conveniently forgetting that she had already seen him several times previously. 'It *must* have been,' she went on. 'I don't usually kiss people on the plane, but I kissed him!'

Out of the blue, at the end of April, Clayton phoned her in New York and proposed. Naomi did not hesitate. She took the next flight out, and Adam was waiting in Dublin with the nouveau-antique 1937 engagement ring which, he joked, had had 'one careful owner'.

'He just popped the question', she said. 'He is a straightforward, down-to-earth person with a lot of love, and he means everything he says. He was very straightforward about it. He understands that there are certain things that we don't have to discuss if I am working late or he's working late. There is just an understanding there. There is a lot of trust between us and that is what I always wanted.'

Asked whether the couple planned to start a family soon, she replied: 'We do want to have a family, but not right now.'

After the show the couple went to celebrate at Dublin's La Tosca restaurant in Suffolk Street, which is owned by Bono's brother Norman Hewson. Their twenty-strong throng then swayed on down to showbiz hangout Lillie's Bordello for a champagne party, which carried on at Adam's home into the early hours.

The next day the couple gave the briefest of photo-calls to newspaper photographers in the driveway of Adam's twenty-room Georgian mansion, which he acquired in 1986 for £300,000, set in 17½ wooded acres near Marlay Park in Rathfarnham, Dublin, next to the boarding school from which he was expelled. After being driven down the 200-yard driveway from the house in a black Jensen sports car, Naomi, dressed in black – bolero jacket, black and white floral-print dress, floppy hat and platform boots – kissed and hugged her fiancé in the pouring rain as lambs frolicked in the fields. It was all too romantic for words.

On the subject of their mile-high first kiss, Adam commented: 'I remember it very well. It was on a plane and it was very nice. You know the way you lean forward and it just happens. There wasn't a time when I realized I loved Naomi – I just knew from the very first moment I saw her.'

Naomi chipped in that she is not marrying Clayton for his money. 'I am not impressed with land and a grand house. It's the person that makes me express my feelings.'

When she was asked why she had announced their engagement on live TV, Clayton interjected: 'Because she does what I tell her!'

They spent the rest of the day celebrating with friends and relatives. Adam's grey-haired Granny Kitty Willis was apparently greatly taken with her grand-daughter-in-law-to-be, and the pair laughed a lot together during the afternoon.

In spite of frantic speculation in the tabloids that the 'Celebrity Wedding of the Year' would take place in secret on Naomi's twenty-third birthday, 22 May, the model was actually working in Paris that day, shooting some additional pictures for the Falmer's jeans campaign using various garments which had not been available at the time of the original shoot. And Adam was on the European leg of U2's tour.

'They are on tour now for four months, six months or maybe even eight months, so between both our schedules we'll have to work it out,' Naomi said later. She then asked her booker Carole White at the Elite Premier agency in London to arrange as many assignments as possible in cities like Paris, Amsterdam and Madrid to coincide with the band's tour dates and enable the couple to be together as often as they could.

And in keeping with the tradition, they look the obligatory odd couple with apparently little in common. He the plain, private musician with the low-key Dublin home life, she the ditsy, flashy spendthrift Supermodel with a des. res. in New York. But we already know the truth about that. That beneath those clashing images beat the kindred hearts of two Black Sheep. That their life-styles, in fact, are indivisible. And the fact that they are only ten years apart in age makes him infinitely more suitable than any of her middle-aged, father-figure beaux. It helps that he is as much the party animal as Naomi. That he travels as extensively as she does, and understands the super-pace lifestyle. And that he performs with the world's greatest band, who throw the best bashes after their live shows, the type of party to which Naomi is automatically invited and loves, but *loves* to attend. As Bono once remarked, 'If rock and roll is a circus, then Adam is in there as the ringmaster. He loves it. He loves it all. He's outlandish and extravagant. He loves fast cars, the rock business, the parties, the life.'

Whether their relationship can endure the long separations,

whether they can contrive to be in the same cities at the same time and prolong the honeymoon period indefinitely, remains to be seen. There will come a time when Naomi's Supermodel career winds down and she will want to spend more time at home. But there is no indication that a true rock and roller ever feels the inclination to quit touring. Not until the Grim Reaper shows his face at the gig.

It perhaps helps enormously that they both hail from this side of the pond, and that they speak the same language. Not in America they don't. If Adam and Naomi still haven't found what they're looking for, then at least they know for sure where they are coming from . . .

Whether or not the marriage ever takes place, the press have been having a field day. Wild speculation about every last detail, from The Dress to the guest list to the bridesmaids to the food, has filled newspaper columns for several months.

On 5 May, the *Sun* devoted half of its Woman's Page to the kind of designers Naomi might consult in her quest for the ultimate frock. 'The 5′ 10″ supermodel will have the pick of Yves St Laurent, Bruce Oldfield and Armani when she marries,' commented the paper knowingly. 'Naomi loves Versace and Gaultier, but her favourite is French designer Azzedine Alaia [he's actually Tunisian], whose style is "pure sex" with body-hugging lines that show off her 34-24-35 figure.'

The *Sun* had then asked three 'top wedding gown designers' to create a dress for the bride. Irish couturier Alison-Jayne had her in a pure white, full-length, off-the-shoulder sheath slashed to the navel to show off her legs, and jewel-encrusted platform ankle-boots. French designer Nicole Manier chose three-tiered transparent organza in pale blue and gold. And London bridal designer Patricia Alison put her in shorts, flowing overskirt and puffy sleeves, making her look more like a Gladiator crossed with a Christmas cake than a blushing bride.

Well, they got one thing right. In May, Naomi did announce that she had chosen 'King of Cling' Azzedine Alaia, who as well as being her favourite designer is also one of her closest friends. It is doubtful whether she will actually have to pay for the dress, which could be worth upwards of £20,000 and is sure to be the antithesis of the traditional wedding gown. It is all but ready – but will it ever be worn? Alaia would of course make it his wedding gift to her. But the designer would reap his share of the rewards. When Elizabeth and David Emmanuel were commissioned to create Lady Diana Spencer's gown for her marriage to Prince Charles, little did they know then how media attention would change their lives. The dress, of course, was seen on television and in newspapers and magazines all over the world. Orders began to flood in from every affluent corner, and the couple were inundated for the best part of a decade before finally dissolving their business and marriage and going their separate ways.

'Marriage A La Mode' gushed the *Daily Express* on 7 May, speculating like mad as to the ins and outs of the Campbell-Clayton union. 'The bride's hair and make-up for the big day certainly won't be a problem. Princess Diana's favourite team of hairdresser Sam McKnight and make-up artist Mary Greenwell, both good friends of Naomi, will be ready to make her look even more beautiful for this special day. Or New York crimper Oribe might fly over on Concorde.'

Photographers? Naomi would be spoilt for choice. 'Princess Diana's favourite Patrick Demarchelier is a likely choice – he recently did pictures of Naomi and her mother for her personal use. But even if he's not taking pictures, Naomi's great friend Steven Meisel – of Madonna *Sex* book fame, who she is currently working with in New York, will be sure to be invited.'

Guest list? It would, they all agreed, be a veritable Who's Who from the worlds of rock and frocks – and of course many were likely to arrive *à deux*: Yasmin and Simon, Helena Christiansen and Michael Hutchence, Linda Evangelista and latest love, *Twin Peaks* star Kyle MacLachlan . . . and maybe even Madonna. But would even this ballsy bride take the risk of inviting the one guest who could surely not resist stealing her thunder . . . ?

The mother of the bride, of course, was in her element following the announcement. Didn't her baby do well? Valerie could barely conceal her pride as she gushed to reporters on 3 May that Adam had gallantly telephoned her to ask for her daughter's hand.

Forty-two-year-old Valerie revealed that Naomi had telephoned her from New York a couple of days before the engagement was announced, saying, 'I've got some news for you, Mum.'

'Is it good news or bad news?' enquired Valerie, somewhat anxiously.

Said Naomi: 'I think you'll like it. Adam has asked me to marry him.'

'She was squealing in delight,' said Valerie. 'She was over the moon. She was thrilled, like any girl would be. I just said, "Lovely, congratulations." About fifteen minutes later, Adam rang me and said, "Mrs Campbell, I would like to ask for your daughter's hand in marriage. I want your permission." It was so romantic, very old-fashioned of him – it is very rare these days. He is a total gentleman. I was quite touched and of course I said "Yes" immediately. He will make a lovely husband for her. He is a lovely man, very down-to-earth, very sweet. They have had,' she remarked wistfully, 'an old-fashioned courtship.'

It is interesting to recall Naomi's words on the subject of love and marriage when I spoke to her in New York. At the time, she owned up to being afraid that men might only want to possess her for her beauty and her body, and not for the real Naomi inside.

'It's a problem for me,' she confessed. 'But then I don't get invited on dates nearly as often as some people imagine. People think that men approach me all the time, and that I am swamped with offers. It's just not true! Are they put off by my image, the fact that I'm well known? They could be. Someone like me, who is so highly visible, it's a bit much for an ordinary guy to take. In a way, it *has* to be someone who has a similar lifestyle to yours, so he understands the pitfalls. Does that mean he has to be rich and famous? Not at all! If I'm having a relationship with someone it's based on love, not financial security.'

Sometimes even love is not enough. Has the Curse of Naomi struck again? Is her longed-for marriage to Adam doomed to go the way of all her other relationships, and will Naomi be left heartbroken and alone yet again?

Could it be that Naomi and Adam actually decided months ago that there was no reason to have a shotgun wedding just to please the newspapers, and that they shrugged off the idea of making a formal announcement, and left the over-excitable media to find out all in good time? Or was this, in fact, a genuine case of eleventh-hour second thoughts, and so one massive headache for whoever was responsible for cancelling the venue, the cake, the guests and the bridesmaids only three weeks before the event?

If they *do* work it out, in time, and decide to marry with the courage of their convictions, we can only wish them luck. It is hard enough to strike a balance in romantic partnerships as it is, without having to do it in the limelight.

Blatant commercialism is never far behind a true love story, especially one involving the rich and famous . . . even in the Emerald Isle. On 16 May 1993, the *Sunday Express* reported that escort and sex service agencies in Ireland were being swamped with calls from clients desperate for the Naomi Campbell experience. 'Customers want Naomi Campbell lookalikes following the model's engagement to U2 star Adam Clayton,' reported the paper. 'Some agencies are flying lookalike lovelies in from Britain because they are so popular.'

In a good Catholic country? The mind could only boggle.

At the Rock 'n' Roll Hall of Fame Gala in Los Angeles with Eric Clapton in January 1993

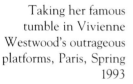

Taking her famous tumble in Vivienne Westwood's outrageous platforms, Paris, Spring 1993

Dancing queen . . .

She gets a kick from
champagne . . .

And on video with Michael Jackson
for his single 'In the Closet'

Above: Supermodel ad for
Vauxhall's new Corsa

A Supermodel has to keep
her fans happy . . .

Mum, didn't we do well!

Happy days with fiancé
Adam Clayton

10

Every Little Thing She Does Is Magic

*T*hrough a faint haze of smog hanging like a damp shroud over Hollywood, the Perfect Face stares down from a vast billboard upon Sunset Boulevard's bumper-to-bumper queue of cars. Three thousand miles away in Times Square the same image pouts from an electronic display board at the legions of New Yorkers scurrying to their jobs. A day away in Barcelona, a trio of young office workers catch sight of it pasted to the side of a bus as they sit eating a lunchtime *bocadillo* beside the Plaza de España fountain. All over Britain, that perfect image looms from the TV set between our favourite programmes. In Tunbridge Wells, a lifesize cardboard cut-out of the same young woman peers knowingly from the window of a jeans store along a dusty side street. On the Champs-Elysées it gazes up at a chic Parisienne from the glossy pages of the *Vogue* magazine she is thumbing through while pausing for a quick *café au lait*. And it gleams from a poster at an elderly black-skirted priest as he strides across the cobbled square towards the Duomo in Milan.

1993 has been nothing if not Naomi's year, her finest hour. A year in which she consolidated her status as a Supermodel as well as proving her worth as an all-round media Superstar. Whatever else they say about her, she is everywhere. And it is not merely her image, but her name. Indeed her very celebrity has all but transformed Naomi from just another pretty face into a brand-name.

Recently the British jeans manufacturer Falmer were quick to pick up on this when they chose Naomi as the body for their brand. They did so not just because of her magical physique, but because she appeared to be the perfect representation of the image that Falmer were seeking to project. It was not merely her looks which inspired them, but her personality and her amazingly high profile, and Falmer are still congratulating themselves on what they consider to be an advertising coup. With the words 'NAOMI CAMPBELL FOR THE FALMER CLOTHING COMPANY' emblazoned across all their ads – *her* name appearing much larger than their own – the Supermodel seems almost to be endorsing the product.

Falmer's spokeswoman Liz Lawley recalls the planning meeting when the idea of using a Supermodel for the campaign was discussed. 'We looked at and discussed all the Supermodels – Linda, Christy, Cindy, all the rest. But we were unanimous in our choice of Naomi. For a start she's British, and so are we – it's unusual for a jeans company to be British. What's more, she didn't have that big, blonde, toothy, beauty-spot look which is so American. Finally, she seemed the one best able to adapt from catwalk glamour to street-style clothes and look equally comfortable in both. We already knew the sort of look we wanted: quite a *hard* look, but without the motorbike – and Naomi turned out to be exactly what we had in mind.'

The original pictures for the campaign were shot in Superstudios, New York, by Canadian photographer Michael Williams, and were widely used as print ads, for in-store promotions and in a poster campaign.

Falmer were not expecting the procedure to be plain sailing, according to Liz Lawley, who says they were prepared for Naomi's legendary lateness, tantrums and general petulant behaviour. 'We had been warned. But she walked in exactly on time, was very friendly, super-professional, extremely cooperative, kind, nice, just lovely to work with. We had her for two days and it went like a dream. We would work with her again.'

As indeed they did, when further photography for the campaign was required for a new set of advertisements, for mail order, and to incorporate various garments which had not been available at the time of the original session. These were shot in a Paris studio, again by Williams, in May 1993.

With such a high-profile advertising campaign, it is usual for someone to object to it. You cannot please all the people all of the time. This Falmer's jeans campaign was no exception, giving rise to accusations that it was offensive to, and derogatory of, women. The principle point of objection appeared to be that the pictures were so blatantly sexual as to be almost pornographic. Those offended had clearly not yet set eyes on the Madonna book. The chief Falmer's shot that was objected to features Naomi wearing nothing but a pair of tiny denim shorts, bondage gloves and leather ankle boots, but her right arm is modestly resting across her breasts. And the epi-centre of the furore was Ireland.

As Liz Lawley confirms, 'There *was* a call for the ads to be banned in Ireland . . . For once we had the press on our side, who thought the objections were absolutely ridiculous. It caused a big stink in Ireland, which served to reflect how behind the times they really are.' The outcome was predictable. 'The Advertising Standards Authority for Ireland were proposing to ban the poster, and upheld the complaints against it,' reports Lawley. 'But due to mounting public pressure, they were forced to reverse their decision.'

Meanwhile, Naomi's personal profile had been rising all the time. By default, the brouhaha had done her fame no harm in the slightest. Particularly as she was now being lovingly embraced as one of Ireland's own daughters . . . this by virtue of the fact that she had become the bride-to-be of one of their most revered rock stars.

It was the Vauxhall car manufacturers who took the process one step further when they launched their new Corsa. By featuring not only Naomi but an entire quintet of Supermodels in a vast, all-embracing campaign, they blatantly exploited their media profile and channelled the association into the hugely successful sale of their own product. The brains behind the sensational campaign belonged to the creative team at Lowe Howard-Spink, one of Britain's top advertising agencies. And a conversation with senior account director Peter Stephenson-Wright is most revealing on the subject of the Supermodels and how the public perceive them.

The concept behind the campaign developed from the look of the car and the beauty of the Supermodels, says Stephenson-Wright. 'The most attractive thing about the car was its looks. It is the thing that strikes you first. It's a much curvier and more stylish car than the others in the small-car sector. And it is aimed at the end of the market which is more about style and personality – the very young, the very independent.'

Through extensive market research over many months, the ad-men got a feel for what the public thought of the Supermodels. Stephenson-Wright explains that the creative team had the brain-wave of using the girls in this campaign when the research revealed just how appealing they were to the car's target audience.

'They represent style and personality and independence, according to our feedback. The thing about getting your own car is that you feel very much that you have taken the world in hand. You are in control of your own life. And one of the aspects of the Super-models, which wasn't so true if you went back twenty or thirty years to the equivalent models then, is that they are seen as being very much in control of their own lives. They have a particular career which, granted, not everyone in every corner of society may approve of. But the main perception seems to be that if this is their job then they do it very well. They are obviously in charge of their lives, and they have made a success of it through their own efforts. These women clearly represent success, good looks and self-deter-mination. Interestingly, nearly everyone was familiar with what a Supermodel is, and they appealed to both men and women across the age groups. It was a complete cross-section.'

When it came to choosing which particular Supermodels would work best in a massive campaign designated for television, hoard-ings, newspapers and magazines, the ad-men found their task was not a hard one. 'There seemed to be seven or eight top Supermodels in the world – there really are no substitutes,' says Stephenson-

Wright. 'We decided to work with four or five, and from there it was a matter of finding out who was available at the right time. We had to shoot them all together as one process, so they had to be around at a certain time.'

The choice came down to Linda Evangelista, Christy Turlington, Tatjana Patitz, British newcomer Kate Moss, and Naomi Campbell. 'For the UK,' he says, 'Naomi was the absolute Number One in terms of recognition and popularity.'

Here began the execution and production of a series of TV commercials and print ads which were controversial and high-profile long before the campaign was launched. An incredible amount of pre-publicity meant that by the time the TV commercial was due to air for the first time – on Thursday, 1 April 1993, during *The Bill* – the public was fully aware that the campaign featured five Supermodels who were all jealous of this new car. *Jealous?*

'Obviously there was a lot of irony and self-mockery intended in the concept,' Stephenson-Wright explains. 'In the original scripts the girls were much more violent towards the car – "The New Supermodel" – but after further research we remodelled these scenes. We made the whole thing much more jokey and ridiculous – that's one of the reasons why it looks so fantastical. They are actually playing out the role of what you'd expect a Supermodel to be.'

Widely reported as being the most expensive campaign in the history of British advertising, with an estimated budget of anywhere between £3 million and £10 million depending on which newspaper you read, and with the individual models being paid anything from £200,000 to £500,000 a head for their input, everybody was talking about the Corsa. The myth was in motion.

'It's actually part of the mythology that surrounds the Supermodels,' says Stephenson-Wright. 'And it reflected superbly on us. The more we denied the sort of amounts of money that were mentioned the bigger it got. Every time we said no, it wasn't five million, it became six. Every time we said no to six, it became twenty million.'

Whatever it cost, the Vauxhall people are not saying. But was Naomi *worth* it? According to Stephenson-Wright, undoubtedly.

'On the shoot itself, Naomi stood out from the others because she seemed the most relaxed of them all, the most sociable. And she probably had the most hazardous conditions to work in. She was enormously helpful and extremely good-natured. The commercial was shot at Shepperton, and we worked to a very tight schedule. Naomi would be in her motor-home being made up. The scene where she appears in a dripping cellar would be set up exactly right with a stand-in playing her role for lighting and movement, and then at the very last minute we'd get her out to play the scene.

'It was a *very* cold day in January, it was below freezing, and the place had a concrete floor so it was extremely chilly. Everyone else was in nineteen layers and coats and things, and here was Naomi dressed in a few strips of leather. They really were hostile filming conditions, but she was utterly professional. It's the one thing you can say about all the Supermodels. They know what they have to do, and they just step out and do the job. If that means walking down a concrete floor on a bitterly cold day dressed in a leather bikini, then that's what they will do. Naomi was superb. And the overwhelming response to the campaign so far says it all.'

What happens when the party's over for a Supermodel like Naomi? When the bubble pops, the cheeks bag and the breasts begin to sag, and nobody thinks you're so super any more? Spare a thought here for all those has-been purveyors of boob-and-ass and eyes-and-teeth, who never did adapt to real life. Who in extreme cases took to the bottle, the syringe, or both, and even wound up back in the gutter from which they had once risen. Or worse, on Tokyo's back streets as a model-turned-prostitute. It happens. For modelling is arguably the last thing that equips you for reality. And short-lived stardom and wealth can be a hell of a price to pay for a pretty face.

Don't think that it never crosses their minds. As much as you may fret over crowsfeet and cellulite, and gravity getting the better of your rump, a model suffers more. Her face and figure are her fortune, and it's not just her loveliness but her living which are at stake. For the average woman, looks aren't everything – not quite. They are only a part of the deal. A model, on the other hand, has everything to lose.

If it's the fame as much as the cash that she is addicted to – and it usually is – she will have considered for some time the possibility of breaking into movies or the music business. In preparation for this, a model takes classes – in everything. Acting tuition, speech therapy, singing lessons, dance sessions, you name it, she's learning it all. In Hollywood they even have a name for it: MTA. It stands for Model-Turned-Actress, and in Tinseltown they are coming at you from every camera angle.

Very few models have actually been able to make the cross-over from the printed page to the silver screen, however, according to Hal Lifson, Executive Producer of Hanna Barbera Productions in Hollywood. 'The problem is that models, by the very nature of their profession, are taught to be *visual* – not on a continual basis but a momentary basis – just for the camera to click,' he says. 'Even the runway performance is only an extended version of that, of them being a larger-than-life version of themselves. It's not acting, it's *attitude*. Strutting. So whenever you see them interviewed they are awkward, they seem gauche, they can't talk and *be* at the same time. They are not used to *being*, but to *posing*.'

A movie, Lifson reminds us, is a series of stills pictures, one after the other, put together. It is not actually moving – but your eye tells you that it *is*. 'A good actress doesn't pose for a frame here, a frame there. She has a whole range of emotions. She doesn't always look perfect when she's crying. And they don't teach you emotional range at acting school, you have to *have* that. What makes an actress interesting and appealing is that she goes up and down in that range. And she's not doing it specifically for the lens. But if the lens manages to captures it, then that is a special moment.

'Demi Moore has range and depth. Michelle Pfeiffer has. Christie Brinkley, on the other hand, was in two movies – briefly. You could see why she wasn't offered a third. They put her as an anchor on CNN for a time, but they whipped her off pretty quick – she was too stiff, too phoney. Cindy Crawford on MTV, though, is something else. She has an unbelievably charming personality, she went to college, she was a good student, she's really good on television, she's unique. But as beautiful as she is at twenty-seven, she knows she will be thirty-seven in ten years . . .

'Jerry Hall was in *Batman* – for five minutes. Madonna is great in a video, but after two hours of watching her in a film you are bored with her. She's all posing, she's *Vogue*. She's spunky, but she needs fire.' Naomi shouldn't look to Madonna for inspiration, Lifson advises: 'She should look to Michelle.'

The main problem that models face when trying to break into Hollywood, he reckons, is that they cannot forget about trying to be pretty all the time. 'A model is taught to look beautiful no matter what. Every expression she makes is meant to be photogenic. Actors, though, do scene-study. They take specialist classes and they try different things by the day. They are ugly as *well* as pretty. They are adaptable. But the thing that you find with a model who wants to be an actress is that she cannot learn to *emote* – good Hollywood word – because she did not have to learn it to be a model.'

The main reason why a good model rarely makes the grade as an actress, then, is that she cannot leave behind what she has learned for the catwalk and the photographic studio and adapt to looking credible in whole scenes. Just as modelling is not nearly as easy as it looks, acting is even harder. According to top photographer and director Terence Donovan, 'Most models cannot act or even deliver one line of dialogue. Because acting is a very, very complex and difficult craft that you have to be taught. The great thing about a model on the still is that it is frozen time. They understand little brief pinnacles of projection. If it's film, it's much more difficult. The toughest thing I get to do is direct a commercial with a beautiful woman delivering dialogue. That's very hard.'

Donovan's advice to models is this: 'Take some acting lessons. Learn the craft. Because the gruesome thing is when they get lucky and get a big commercial. You can't get away with just pouting for the lens then. It's a bit more complex than rock and roll!'

The model who believes she will land a lucrative Hollywood contract on the strength of her beauty alone is seriously deluded. The reality, for 90 per cent of them, is very different from the dream. As Hal Lifson explains, 'A lot of the time, models are simply *too* attractive. There is therefore a lack of accessibility. They are chiselled to perfection, they are always working on their looks. They are not just beautiful women, they are awesome. This tends to make them completely unapproachable as people – they seem "cold" on screen somehow, and uninviting. They do not draw you in because they look too good to be human. From a man's point of view, on a sexual and physical level, what could be better than a model?'

But true sensuality, emotion and bonding, he agrees, comes from within. 'An actress needs *all* those qualities,' Lifson affirms. 'But the majority of models are stupid – they are not that bright. Why? Because they don't need to be. Not until the looks begin to fade. Think about the typical model's day. She might go to the gym and work out a little, she gets a massage, she gets her nails done, she goes shopping. It all gets pretty shallow after a while. You think she reads the papers and watches the news? The hell she does! But good actresses develop themselves intellectually. Models tend not to bother, because at the time they don't need to, then they make a big song and dance about improving themselves later on.'

Name ten former models who have made it as actresses. You can't? You have just proved Lifson's point. The Supermodels, however, rattle off all the names they can think of like a litany. 'Jessica Lange was a model,' Naomi argued when we had this discussion. 'Ali McGraw, Cybill Shepherd, Brooke Shields, Marisa Berenson, Candice Bergen, Lauren Hutton, Andie MacDowell, Geena Davis, Rene Russo,' she recited.

It was Twiggy herself who started the MTA syndrome – though she didn't know it at the time – when she retired from the catwalk and launched herself as an actress, first in Ken Russell's charming twenties' musical picture *The Boy Friend* in 1971, the year after Naomi was born, and later on Broadway in Tommy Tune's *My One and Only*. She went on to star with Shirley MacLaine in the movie *Madame Souzatska*, and has carved a respectable career in film and television. But in the meantime, where was Jean Shrimpton? Far from trying to cash in on her sixties' profile, the David Bailey favourite simply faded away to Cornwall where she established a small country hotel.

Naomi finds it hard to believe that models are judged so harshly for trying to branch out into showbiz. 'Now that models like Iman (Mrs David Bowie) and Paulina Porizkova (the Face of Estee Lauder) are trying it, they are having such a hard time. But *why?* It's not fair. Just because you are successful in one field, and you become highly visible and even popular as a result, that shouldn't mean you can't try your hand at something else. You shouldn't have to be labelled to do just one job the whole of your life. Why *not* try something else?

'It seems to me that this whole thing is to do with the fact that it's a stigma to have a pretty face and a good body. It's like you're not *allowed* to have everything – you can't be talented as well! I'm not saying I've got everything – God! But you can certainly try other things, and that's all I'm trying to do. You have to pick up your feet and have a go. But you are criticized for that. I think it's sad.'

Paulina Porizkova agrees: 'Today, everybody's an MTA!' she laughs. 'People think the term's synonymous with no talent no brain. We know different.'

It is worth remembering – before one stoops to ridicule Naomi for cashing in on Supermodel fame by seeking to conquer the worlds of music and movies – that showbiz was what Naomi was trained for in the first place. 'This is not what my mother spent all her money on sending me to school for,' she said about her burgeoning model career. However, she was the first to admit that she'd have been some fool not to take that opportunity when it knocked.

When she first arrived in New York Naomi still took dancing classes whenever she could, but a frantic schedule got the better of her. The one person she always made time for, however, was her speech coach. And of course she'd chosen Manhattan's finest.

Sam Chwat, a linguistic scientist, professional speech therapist and dialect coach of fifteen years' standing, came highly recommended. Robert De Niro, Sean Young, Kathleen Turner, Julia Roberts and Cindy Crawford are just a handful of his grateful celebrity clients – their gushing tributes are emblazoned across his walls – all of whom visited their 'voice guru' at his New York Speech Improvement Services studio on 16th Street. Chwat taught Kathleen Turner a Southern accent for her role as Maggie in *Cat on a Hot Tin Roof*, knocked the Irish out of Patrick Bergin for *Sleeping with the Enemy*, and brought Cindy Crawford's pitch down a peg or two for her performance in a Revlon Flex shampoo commercial.

With Naomi however, it was back to basics. '*Why* does she want to learn an American accent? For the same reason as everybody else,' Chwat told me. 'To make it in Hollywood, which she plans to do, you must first acquire a general, standard, unremarkable American accent – the kind that was developed somewhere between Madison Avenue and Hollywood and which doesn't actually exist anywhere. Which is, in fact, a rather sloppy and corrupt brand of mutilated English! The accent is simply another article of clothing to wear. I call it "choreography of the mouth". Seeking to develop an American accent has nothing to do with your attitudes, nor your feelings towards Americans. It is simply a style.'

Naomi felt that her London accent was a stigma, remembers Chwat. 'Oh, you're so cute, you sound charming, never lose your accent – it's *adorable*, they'd all say to her,' he laughs. 'But it wasn't going to get her the *roles*. There are very few parts in Hollywood which require British accents. Butlers and Nazi officers, traditionally – though don't ask me about the German connection, I have no idea.'

Sam reports that Naomi was an excellent pupil. 'We've been working on the Ts, the Ds, the – INGs – she leaves those off quite frequently!' he told me when I met him in the summer of 1992, and Naomi was still attending sessions regularly. 'She's pretty good about her Hs, but her Rs are definitely a problem.

'I do see quite a lot of models. It is normal for someone like Naomi to want to expand her options. Modelling is an unpredictable and short-lived career. She wants to make herself available for film, TV and commercials, the whole range. She is considered a very exotic type here. Being black, wearing those wigs, varying her look, being this *wonderful* creature she is quite hard to cast, so she needs to make herself adaptable. But she will do whatever it takes, believe me. She's committed.

'She did in fact get work on this black sitcom, *Fresh Prince of Bel Air*, for ABC TV – she played a gorgeous black au pair, and they specifically requested her British accent. But that's not enough for her – of course not. She has her eye on the big-time.'

More power to her, reckons Chwat, who was clearly impressed with her professionalism and application: 'They say she doesn't get out of bed for less than $10,000 a day. But when she *does*, she comes here to see me first! I'd often see her before 8 a.m. She has a very busy schedule – she's always catching a plane – but she would always make time to come to her lessons, and she was very conscientious.

'I wish her well. She's fun, she's diligent, we get along very well. The only problem I can really see for her is practice. Many British people in America are really very reluctant to try out their new accent socially, because they get so much mileage out of their native one!'

They succumb eventually, it would seem. For an all-American accent is not just a trick of the trade, but in some cases the essence of a new identity. As Sam Chwat remarks, 'People living here in America, far away from their family and friends, are free to be and do whatever they want. They can reinvent themselves totally if they wish. It can be a game. No one knows who you are, you could be *anybody*. You new accent becomes part of the mask you have chosen to wear.'

Accents speak louder than words. Naomi, as yet, does not appear to have perfected the Hollywood-friendly version. When engaged in conversation with her, you notice that hers swings from Streatham High Road to Fifth Avenue to Sunset Boulevard and back again. Her speech is a combination of modern London and New York vernacular, downtown rap, Supermodel babble, occasional vulgarities and the odd sophisticated phrase she has appropriated along the way. The accent varies accordingly. This is partly because she is still so young, but also because, in common with many who travel extensively and have a 'musical ear', she is a victim of what she hears. As she tours the world, her subconscious is endlessly bombarded with the sound of the English language in all its glorious diversity. Cosmopolitan conversation with a pantheon of foreign colleagues would bring out the chamelon in any of us – at the expense of the constant. Stabilizing the requisite accent is therefore rendered all the more difficult for the Exotic Stray.

Does Naomi have what it takes to make it beyond the catwalk? There is no doubt in the mind of New York fashion stylist and movie costume designer Pené, who first met her at a Manhattan hairdressing salon, forged a loose friendship with her, and has watched her career ever since.

'She's a workaholic – and she demands efficiency,' Pene told me. 'Naomi is very special. Nothing about her success surprises me. She works harder than anybody I know. I'm talking about getting on planes when she is too sick to travel. Looking a million dollars on the runway when she is totally depressed. There is a lot more to come, believe me. Naomi is a great performer, and she will take that into her music and then into Hollywood. And then, in whichever direction she wants to go.'

When we spoke, Pene had been working with Aleta Chappelle, a respected Hollywood casting director, on Eddie Murphy's movie

Boomerang. She and Chappelle had a conversation about acting, and Pene quizzed her on Naomi Campbell's chances. Chappelle admitted that she had been watching Naomi develop over the past few years, and commented: 'She has actually gotten better and better. I think she is going to make a *great* actress.'

'This, let me tell you,' added Pené, 'is not a woman to make statements.'

For as long as anyone can remember, Naomi has had 'an album coming out in the spring'. Over the past four years, press reports and even exclusive interviews have been hinting at the sensational sounds she has been working on with music business luminaries such as Virgin Records' Jeff Ayeroff, who was responsible for the success of Paula Abdul and Neneh Cherry; Madonna's former producer Jellybean Benitez; Michael Jackson's long-time guru Quincy Jones' and a whole harmonious host of others.

Her records, curiously, never materialize. She has been heard, briefly, on a Vanilla Ice single, but to date that has been about it in terms of output. Naomi, meanwhile insists to all and sundry that she is 'working on her album'. That she is 'putting the brakes on her modelling career to concentrate on recording'. That she is now going to turn her attention to her music 'more or less full-time'.

She surely meant it, every sentence, at the time. The simple fact is that her life is not that simple. Take this year, for example. On 5 April 1993, the very day I arrived in New York to research this book, Naomi was due in a Manhattan studio booked by her management at Sony Inc. to start recording an album. The record company, formerly CBS Records incorporating Epic and sundry other labels before it was acquired by the Japanese manufacturing conglomerate, announced that they were confident they would have an entire album by Naomi Campbell written, recorded, produced, packaged and ready to market by October 1993. Sony executives both in New York and in London spoke to me in glowing terms of the high hopes they had for Naomi, not only as a recording artist but as a marketing man's dream. Not only can she sing – she has this *incredible* voice, I was assured – but she was a publicist's gift. Which we all knew already.

To look at? To *die* for! Dances like a dream – undulated *rings* around Michael Jackson in the video for his single 'In the Closet' from the *Dangerous* album, which was directed by Naomi's bosom buddy lensman Herb Ritts in the Californian desert in 1992.

Said photographer Phil Ramey, who watched Naomi throw her bare legs around 'The Gloved One's' waist and grind her body against his as he took exclusive pictures of the sex-rated romp on set: 'Naomi really went for it – and you could see that Michael was rather taken aback!'

As for Naomi, she had a *ball* on set, and even found time to play a practical joke on Jackson before he had a chance to pull one of his favourite stunts on *her*. 'Michael's a really nice person,' she gushed. 'He was very professional – when it came time for action we both did what we were told to do. But whatever else he was planning, I got in first – and absolutely soaked him with some water bottles I got hold of after the shoot.' As they say in the biz, Who's Bad?

As for the promotion of Naomi Campbell's own album, those very nice Sony people could do it with their mouths shut. In fact, it would probably do itself. She would never have to do the leg work, the pub-and-club circuit with a band. Rather than creep on to the music scene the way most new artists have to, she would burst on to it with a bang. The music press, the national newspapers, the teen magazines, not to mention the chat show hosts and radio DJs, would all be falling over themselves to interview her. For once, they would have a legitimate excuse to talk *to* the girl that everybody talks *about*.

Naomi's recording deal with Sony was actually signed with the American company, in New York. But in London, more than any-where else, they could barely contain their excitement.

'This will be a very important release for us,' confided one senior

Sony executive. 'Naomi Campbell is someone with an international name – she is known all over. I have never actually heard
her sing, and I don't know what she can do,' he admitted. 'This may
sound terrible, but it provides us with a great marketing opportunity
in this changing music industry which we really can't afford to miss.
This *is* a new venture for her. But she's a known commodity, a
household name. Unless she falls off a bridge or gets hit by a truck, I
would say that chart success for Naomi is more or less guaranteed.'

Back in New York, they were tossing slightly less caution to the
wind. 'We are *not* planning to put out this album until we have a
very strong feeling that it is amazing,' an American Sony executive
told me. 'Yes, it is hard to pin her down. She has the craziest
schedule, and no one controls her. It seems she really is her own
boss. It can make life difficult,' he said diplomatically. Especially, in
other words, for record company people who love more than anything to call the shots.

A month later Sony were having to admit that not only was
recording behind schedule, it had not even started. 'Nothing's been
done. She is sick,' I was informed. 'She's had a bad cold. Her voice
is not really ready. The doctors are calling the shots.'

While many of us await her CD with bated breath, there are others
who seem underwhelmed by the idea of a Supermodel launching
herself as a recording artist. TV producer Chips Chipperfield, who
worked on many rock and pop videos for Picture Music International before going on to produce specials for Tina Turner, Nigel
Kennedy and Paul McCartney and who is currently masterminding
the Beatles anthology, believes it is regrettable that so much money
is channelled into launching a model as an artist when there are so
many needy and worthy bands out there who simply cannot get a
break.

'It's a terrible shame,' he says. 'Just because she is famous, she gets
given it on a plate. On the other hand, if she has got talent, she
should do it – and good luck to her. I notice that Naomi has been

criticized for being signed for her looks and not her singing or song-writing talent. But that's pretty well always been the case, if truth be told. Look Right is more important than Sound Right. Sound you can fix. Even the Beatles came via that route. They could play a *bit* in the beginning – but more importantly they *looked* great. Their songwriting skills came later. MTV [America's Music Television pop and rock channel] is largely to blame. Because of it, imagery has become more important than the music. It has done a great disservice to the music business.'

It all boils down, Chips says, to marketing: 'Record companies market product, that's all. It's not about art any more. Samantha Fox did it first, didn't she? Tit and roll! And Whitney Houston. So Naomi Campbell wants to do a Whitney. Who's writing her songs? Well, with the right machinery they can make anyone sing. It's because of stuff like this that, slowly but surely, the record industry is screwing itself into the ground.'

It's an opinion. But it is probably more true to say that even electronics cannot disguise a poor voice – and that a quality voice will always shine.

She's everywhere and nowhere, baby. She's where it's at. A movie with Mel? A duet with Jacko? Well, the whole world for an oyster and time enough to have a crack at the lot, at least.

Back at her old school, Barbara Speake and June Collins are cautious in their assessment of Naomi's chances of making it as a pop star. As Miss Speake points out, with characteristic bluntness: 'It does not follow that a record will be a raging success because it's someone famous making it. Being well known does not ensure success in another field. If they don't like the music they won't buy it – simple as that. A lot depends on hype, on the publicity that surrounds it. She's got the ability, she's a good singer, she *could* do it. But there's more to it than that. June always says, "Be *nice*. It's contagious." Her son Phil Collins, of course, is very, *very* nice . . . in fact, he's heartily sick of being called Mr Nice Guy. But it's always worth remembering to be respectful to the press, which he is. The press can slaughter you, and no mistake. If you are not popular with them, they can definitely break you – they've done it hundreds of times.'

Miss Speake is the first to acknowledge that her former pupil certainly looks good, and ought to sound good on record, too. But she warns that a lot depends on the material she is given – the actual songs. 'Then of course she will have to tour – and that's bloomin' hard work, as Phil will tell you any day. He was really shattered at the end of this last tour. She won't like touring – she's not all that strong, she's quite a fragile girl. And it is a lot harder for a girl, by the way. It takes its toll. And another thing: will the voice hold up?'

June Collins' advice to Naomi would be to concentrate on a film career rather than try to make it as a pop singer. 'She should forget about a recording career – there are so many in it already, and girls like her are two a penny. I'm not being rude, it's perfectly true. They all get it wrong. It is not just a question of looking the part and then putting out a few records. It's a really hard graft. And I should know – I'm a rock and roll Mum! I would say, stick to what she is really good and successful at – at least until she is too old to do it – and *then* try for a good film. She is so beautiful, so successful, she's commanding all this big money. She's got everything going for her, and she should make the most of it while she can.'

It *is* possible for a Face to become a Voice, of course. Whitney Houston was a model before she got the hang of opening her mouth (after which there was no stopping her). And Vanessa Williams, a former Miss America, achieved massive musical stardom in a market which certainly does not suffer fools. Her debut release sold 800,000 copies in the USA and her album *The Comfort Zone* went to number one on the R & B charts.

'Yet I still hear people say, "Oh, she's just getting ahead on her looks,"' Vanessa laments. 'People don't *see* your looks when they're listening to the radio and requesting your songs! Beauty might make people notice you, but it doesn't make them buy your records. It actually does come from within, anyway. And attitude, brains and talent are worth much more than looks alone.' It is perhaps an easy statement to make when you look as fabulous as she does.

A number of music business executives I consulted on Naomi's chances as a recording artist were in full agreement with her former teacher, Barbara Speake – that what will really make or break her is the quality of her songs. After that, much will depend upon how exactly her record company positions her releases in the market. A hit single in the UK is one thing, which these days probably does not count for much. And the United States is such a huge, fragmented market with endless charts and dozens of categories that you have got to pitch your product exactly right in order to make any kind of impact.

What will be the flavour of Naomi's music? Rap? Soul? R & B? Pop? Rock? Dance? Black? A cross-over combination? Or even, God forbid, MOR? Or will Sony approach this project in the same way that Arista Records handled their prize artist Whitney Houston's first album? Not to everyone's taste, it was nevertheless a masterpiece in the 'All Things To All People' category, constructed in such a way that various tracks could be lifted from it at random and fed to each of the individual shards of the singles market in order to stimulate album sales as a whole.

Whether Naomi's backers go for this type of broad-spectrum appeal, or decide instead to make it more specific, they have got to get it right. Then again, not necessarily first time. Naomi is a big enough star to be afforded at least a couple of cracks at the whip. For it is a fact that she will have more opportunity to succeed than most of us get in a lifetime. Her modelling career has guaranteed that.

But let us not forget that she has also been trained as an entertainer, a dancer, and a singer, and knows how to deal with the lens in whatever form it confronts her. It seems likely that, if Sony get her material and the marketing position right, Naomi herself will do the rest. A recording career, of course, can only happen as the result of the efforts of a very full complement of staff. So if it does backfire, it will not necessarily be her fault. And if her team *do* get it wrong, you can be sure that the hacks will once again be waiting in the wings with the sharpened laptops . . .

It is perhaps reasonable to suggest that she has nothing to fear. She's well trained, she's professional, she works hard, she's always into something new, and she of all people would relish the challenge. This is not the beginning of the end for a Supermodel – rather the end of the beginning for an international showbusiness star. She is sure to be massive . . . watch this space!

In the inimitable words of Hanna Barbera's Hal Lifson, 'She'll *do* it! Naomi will be an *incredibly* big star, and will take over where Diana Ross left off. She'll do it if only because we need a black female megastar who doesn't look like Whoopi Goldberg. It's called timing.'

Epilogue

Karma Chameleon

Manhattan, Friday afternoon. For what seems like the first time in an age, Naomi finds herself hanging out in her own apartment. Would you believe it? It has been another typical week: Miami on Monday, Madrid Tuesday, London Wednesday, Paris Thursday, then back to New York. She is home for just twelve hours – tomorrow morning she departs for St Martin in the Caribbean islands for a weekend shoot, and God *knows* where Concorde will take her next.

'Thank God my agency can ask for first class or Concorde now is all I can say, or I would be dead by now,' laments the ultimate Supermodel. 'It's been a plane every day, and these are not short trips, you know? Everyone thinks I lead such a glamorous lifestyle, but I seem to spend more time in airport lounges and in airplane toilets than I ever do at wild parties!'

The jet-set lifestyle is rarely what it seems. Nevertheless, Naomi has the choice – and for now, she chooses to be doing it. After all, her Supermodel status is more likely to give her up than the other way around. She knows enough to make the most of it while she can. She'll play the game, set the scene, be the perfect Supermodel from shorn roots to lacquered toenails.

On Concorde she will slurp water and sleep, surrounded by all her 'bags of junk' to which British Airways benevolently turn a blind eye. In Paris she'll be nicer than pie to everyone at the Ritz. On the catwalks of Milan she'll strut her stuff, thinking, 'Fuck you, fuck you, fuck *you*!' as she works the room, smouldering down on jaded fashion editors and buyers in their Chanel jackets and dark glasses, which experience tells them to wear to shield their eyes from the blazing lights, but which they might as well be wearing to protect themselves from the very dazzle of *her*. In the dressing rooms and make-up suites she will snatch half an hour of sleep under a table, munch an apple, get stuck into a book, help the dressers and make-up artists as much as possible to make her look nothing less than perfect. Naomi will be everything that is expected of her – and only by such efforts can she be everything she is expected to be. And she will have been having exactly the same conversation all over the world!

'Because the fashion circus is constantly on the move – not just the designers but the photographers, store buyers, fashion editors and models – it creates its own homogeneous society, at once international and profoundly xenophobic,' says Nicholas Coleridge in his book *the Fashion Conspiracy*. 'A buyer for a New York store will fly two hundred thousand miles a year from fashion capital to fashion capital, inspecting collections, but she will eat at the same few restaurants and discuss the same tiny cast of characters . . . the larger the fashion industry grows, the fewer the players that really count . . . it is scarcely surprising, with such a tiny nucleus of opinion-makers hurtling around the world, that the level of paranoia is so high.'

'A lot of people think it's this glamorous cushy life, but there is a downside to it,' one leading fashion editor told me. 'There's not a lot of depth involved. Models are not the most soulful of people, and they must think about that sometimes. Think about it yourself: if you come straight out of school at sixteen into modelling, all you ever do is chit-chat and talk about hair and clothes and make-up. Models get really annoyed when we say they are stupid, but I'm sorry, most of them *are*. People like me get very annoyed when a model expresses an opinion about the clothes we are asking them to wear. That is not their job, and we shut them up. I suppose we encourage them to be a little bit mute, none of which helps. Then they are coddled like mad because you don't want them to start crying, as the make-up will have to be redone. And everybody is telling them how beautiful they are, how wonderful, darling, because you want them to feel good – it's all a terribly false existence, they must wonder sometimes what people *really* think of them. They are not that stupid that they don't *care.*'

And yes, some of them take drugs to keep going: 'I did a show recently with about twenty girls, and they all disappeared just before they were due to go on, and their expressions were very different when they came back,' said Lowri Turner. 'I blame the parents, who allow their fourteen-year-old children to start on this life. It's very dangerous – because they get used to Having It All early on, it's so much harder for them to come back down to the real world.'

A modelling career, for most girls, is over by the time they hit twenty-four. It's a hell of a young age to be a has-been, and a comedown that many of them never quite get the hang of. One minute they are earning enormous amounts of money, and the next they're unemployed. They have for so long been used to having everything paid for, everything free, their first-class travel, their limousines to take them everywhere, their swish hotel suites . . . and suddenly they are out there in the cold, not knowing how to fend for themselves. They are not trained for anything else, they no longer have the capacity to earn that kind of money, they no longer count.

'What most of them do is find a man, *any* man, get pregnant as quickly as they can and have the baby,' says Lowri Turner. 'And then they find that it's not all that glamorous having a kid, so they try to get back into modelling, but by this time they are past it . . . it's hard not to feel sorry for them.'

According to photographer Terry O'Neill: 'The public just don't realize how hard they work. They'll jump on a plane, go to Milan, go to bed, get up really early, do four fittings, do six shows a day for a week, no spare time whatsoever, jump on a plane, go back to New York, get up really early, do a modelling assignment. It's non-stop. I'm amazed the top girls have any private life at all. They work harder than Olympic athletes. Naomi is the best at it – she's there on the phone with her diary on her lap while she's having her make-up done, making appointments, running her life and her business affairs at the same time as getting ready to be photographed. She's always doing twenty things at once. You've got to admire her.'

Terry, for one, wonders how models manage to retain their sanity through all the madness and the chaos of their lifestyles. 'A girl becomes a model, she's sweet and unspoilt and everyone says "Aah, she's adorable." She gets famous, she moves up, she's supposed to remain sweet and unspoilt, but how you actually *can* . . . when at sixteen you are travelling all around the world on your own. Of all the models I know, there's not a single one I would regard as sane . . . the same goes for photographers, by the way! This life itself is enough to make anyone lose a tile from their roof. Apart from all the travel and never knowing where you are from one day to the next, it's a very lonely job. You are constantly going for the next thing, and the next, and they've got to keep their weight down, and worry about the crowsfeet – it's *crazy.*'

It is a lifestyle which soon separates the Supermodels from the girls. A Supermodel, for example, is always ready to face the press. At 7.30 a.m. she's already wearing a light coat of foundation and her dark glasses – just in *case*. 'And the ultimate accessory,' says American *Vogue*'s creative director André Leon Talley, 'is for a model to have her own camera crew.'

If ever a girl had reason to be disenchanted by fame, it would appear to be Naomi. It is a *mad* life. How on earth can she be expected to make sensible decisions about her future when she has never had a settled existence? How should she make order out of chaos, create a structured and fulfilling relationship and even marry and have a family when the very career she is pursuing continues to drag her to opposite ends of the earth? Models, after all, do not have a great track record in the matrimonial department. Twiggy's heart was broken several times before she eventually found happiness, well into her thirties, with actor Leigh Lawson. Marie Helvin could not hold it together with David Bailey. The marriages of both Linda Evangelista and Christy Turlington have dissolved in the spotlight. Yasmin le Bon, on the other hand, has created a cosy home life with Simon and their two children, and Jerry Hall has hung on to Mick and all the little Jaggers by the skin of her teeth, in spite of her husband's numerous infidelities. Models, by virtue of their beauty, fame and wealth, do not automatically live happily ever after. Like princesses and ordinary mortals, they have to work at it.

Still, you have to admire Naomi for hanging on to her sanity in spite of being what she is: the world's most talked-about Supermodel. A considerable part of her headline-making propensity is the result of her extraordinary visibility. She cannot hide. Naomi incognito is a contradiction in terms. Everyone knows and recognizes her face, her legs, her mouth, her sexy pout. Wherever she goes she is on public display, and few if any of her antics go unnoticed. Almost everyone from her world has a Naomi Campbell anecdote to tell. Like all legends, hers has a strong vein of truth in it – and an equally strong vein of fiction. How appropriate that she should now have been contracted by a publisher to the tune of a reported £100,000 to 'write' a fictional account of her own life story. A novel idea if ever there was one.

In the end, we cannot say that we know all there is to know about her, any more than we could say the same about our own friends. She and her career are evolving all the time. But the appeal of this unique woman remains constant. Perhaps Hollywood will one day make a film about her life and times, especially if she makes it as a pop or film star: a terrible sort of B-movie starring someone too young to remember Naomi in her heyday, a movie which will troll out all the myths, extend them to grossly illogical conclusions, and then invent a few more. It is not as unlikely as it seems. No Supermodel ever looked like Naomi, or behaved like Naomi, or had such a colourful, explosive life. Most Supermodels should be seen and not heard, and most of them *are*, and most of them fade into obscurity. There is little doubt that, whatever career she chooses to pursue when her modelling days are over, whether as singer or actress or TV chat show host or all of these, Naomi will be around for the duration. Obscurity is definitely not for her.

The legend is embellished by the day. On 10 July 1993, America's MTV featured a special one-hour Supermodel summit on its *House of Style* show, hosted by Cindy Crawford. In the weeks leading up to its airing, *everybody* was talking about it: what the models were wearing, what they said, the fact that they filmed the piece in the upstairs room at Robert De Niro's TriBeCa Grill, that Naomi's cappuccino went cold as her cellular phone rang incessantly, even while she was being interviewed for television! Naomi, coming on like a dippy flower child for the nineties, insisted that Supermodels are *not* superhuman beings – but we knew that anyway. 'We have no special powers,' she trilled. Which is of course the point. Pre-publicised to the hilt and billed as the summer's hippest show, repeated over and over again on MTV, the programme had to be a sure-fire hit, offering as it did half a dozen beautiful models with household names to an audience ever hungry for glamour. Who cares about what they didn't really have to say?

Naomi, interrogated by Cindy on the subject of her sexuality and whether she felt it was being abused, claimed that she doesn't feel sexy, but gawky! In her giggly-shy little girl voice, she said she never gets hit on by men – that indeed, most men seem intimidated by her larger-than-life Supermodel image. And she and Cindy reminisced about the time they met for dinner in a London restaurant, and two women at an adjacent table stared on enviously as the slender models took their seats and signalled to the waiter that they were ready to order. Deciding there and then to play a practical joke, Naomi and Cindy ordered two dinners each, a huge plate of French Fries, chocolate cake, and demolished the *lot*. Naomi, of course, would happily waltz away without gaining one ounce, she can eat anything. Poor Cindy, on the other hand, was the first to admit that she simply cannot compete, and would have to exercise flat-out for a week to counteract the ill-effects of such a gluttonous prank.

Naomi, admitting for the first time that she owed her 'big break' in the US to photographer Steven Meisel opened up on a number of other subjects. The fact that her formal education was cut short appears to bug her: she said that, as she had travelled and seen the world, she got her education that way. And she was the only one to look suitably nervous and embarrassed when the question of Super-models intimidating the younger, upcoming models was raised. While the others, including veteran Lauren Hutton and Linda Evangelista, denied being bitchy and difficult, Naomi admitted that she is sometimes guilty of this.

You know you have made it when they hold up a film premiere until you arrive. For Naomi, incredibly, they did just that. When *The Night We Never Met* had its New York debut this summer, Naomi Campbell found herself running late. And the organizers delayed the screening until she got there. Even royalty would not expect such a privilege, nor take such a liberty. In Greenwich Village's Webster Hall for the after-premiere jaunt, Naomi's 'What can I say?' grin said it all.

At an after-show party one night, you run into Naomi Campbell's mother. Naomi is not the only one who has come a long way from Streatham High Road, that's for sure. Get *Valerie*: the picture of elegance in a chic black suit, her silk hair curling down over her shoulders, her designer make-up perfect, her skin even better than her famous daughter's. Her smile says Cat Got The Cream. Her eyes beam Didn't We Do Well. Daughter has done a grand job of fulfill-ing Mother's dreams – although you can't help hoping that Naomi has fulfilled her own ambitions too.

You can hardly blame Valerie: it's a rare mother who has the looks and confidence to launch her own modelling career on the back of her daughter's, but at forty-two, Valerie is probably as glamorous a mother as you can get. Nevertheless, she insists, she will only accept modelling assignments in keeping with her age and image: 'I don't want to rival my daughter, and I would never do catwalk modelling,' she insists. 'I don't want to wear the kind of things that Naomi wears. That would be mutton dressed as lamb. But there isn't a black woman of my age out there doing it, so I thought, if I can do it, then I will.'

Meanwhile, she's out there in her element, rubbing shoulder pads with the Lawsons, the Eklands, the Kilroy-Silks. And she has, apparently, embarked on her autobiography: it is time to debunk a few myths – and, perhaps, to launch one or two new ones.

Back in London, the beautifully preserved Campbell *mère* was seen dining out with the portly, mega-rich Duke of Northumberland, whose friendship she appears to have energetically cultivated, apparently discussing a role for herself in one of his Hotspur film company's forthcoming features. The supper, it's said, was at *her* invitation. What the hell, he turned *up*. The Campbell dream, finally, has come full circle.

Index